WHAT PEOPLE ARE SAYING ABOUT
THE MARRIAGE YOU'VE ALWAYS DREAMED OF

"This delightful book is packed with powerful ideas for helping you enter the full promise of your marriage. By bringing you rich insights to the story of how God freed the Israelites from bondage and by offering practical strategies and skills, Greg Smalley shows you how God can bring your marriage into freedom. Read it and be blessed."

SCOTT M. STANLEY
professor at University of Denver, coauthor of *A Lasting Promise*

"With this remarkable book, Dr. Greg Smalley will take your marriage to a destination you've only dreamed possible. Filled with powerful and practical insights, *The Marriage You've Always Dreamed Of* is your guidebook on the most important journey you'll ever take."

DRS. LES AND LESLIE PARROTT
professors at Seattle Pacific University, authors of *The Love List*

"God wants your marriage relationship to grow and flourish. Greg provides insights and tools so that couples can take conflicts and change them into steps of growth. This book will equip you to make your good marriage better or help your struggling marriage to soar. If you read this book and apply just 10 percent of what Greg shares, you'll benefit for the rest of your lives together!"

DENNIS RAINEY
president of FamilyLife and host of *FamilyLife Today*

"I've read literally hundreds of books about relationships, and this one is unique. It is packed with fresh ideas and practical suggestions that have been forged in the real-life experiences of the author. My wife, Carrie, and I have watched Greg and Erin go through courtship and the early years of marriage and parenting to build a strong, healthy, and vibrant Christ-centered marriage. Just learning about the Fear Dance is worth the price of the book. If you are willing to learn a new dance, God could use it to take your marriage to the next level. Greg has given all of us who are married a significant book that will be around for a long time. Give yourself or someone you love the gift of this book!"

GARY J. OLIVER, TH.M., PH.D.
executive director of the Center for Marriage and Family Studies and professor of psychology and practical theology at John Brown University, coauthor of *Raising Sons and Loving It!* and *Good Women Get Angry*

"For those of us seeking to improve the well-being of children by rebuilding a culture of marriage, *The Marriage You've Always Dreamed Of* is a most welcome tool for helping couples form and sustain healthy marriages."

THE HONORABLE WADE F. HORN, PH.D.

"Using powerful biblical metaphors of the Israelites' deliverance to the Promised Land, Greg Smalley creatively encourages couples to persevere with faith, love, and the skills to meet their marital goals. A master storyteller, Greg uses humorous anecdotes from his own marriage, as well as his wealth of clinical experience, to give couples insight and practical ideas in building a successful marriage. Greg Smalley's dream and passion for a marriage revival are visionary and contagious! His passion parallels that of his father and leaves the reader with not only the faith that a marriage revival is possible but also the desire to sign on as an advocate! *The Marriage You've Always Dreamed Of* delivers couples to a great marriage!"

DAVID H. OLSON, PH.D.
president of Life Innovations, author of *Empowering Couples*

"If we needed heart surgery, we'd head to the Mayo Clinic. If we needed marriage therapy, we'd head to the Mayo Clinic of marriages: the Smalley Marriage Institute, where the tools in this book are practiced daily. This book is just what the doctor ordered, whether your marriage needs a complete physical, major surgery, or just a consult. We guarantee your marriage will be well cared for as you pursue the principles in *The Marriage You've Always Dreamed Of.*"

DR. GARY AND BARBARA ROSBERG
cohosts of *America's Family Coaches—LIVE!* and authors of *Divorce-Proof Your Marriage*

"Just as the wilderness journey brought struggles but the manifestation of God's faithfulness—so Greg Smalley has shown us how God can give us grace in struggles common to all God's people. We, too, trek through 'this great and terrible wilderness' into the Promised Land. Easy, relevant, biblical. A blessing to any who take of this manna."

TOMMY NELSON
senior pastor of Denton (Texas) Bible Church and
author of *The Book of Romance*

YOU ARE
CORDIALLY INVITED TO

the
Marriage
You've Always
Dreamed
Of

_____
HUSBAND
_____

_____
WIFE

THE MARRIAGE YOU'VE ALWAYS DREAMED OF

a book in

THE DNA OF RELATIONSHIPS CAMPAIGN

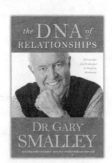

DR. GREG SMALLEY

the
Marriage
You've Always
Dreamed
Of

Tyndale House Publishers, Inc.
Wheaton, Illinois

Visit Tyndale's exciting Web site at www.tyndale.com

TYNDALE is a registered trademark of Tyndale House Publishers, Inc.

Tyndale's quill logo is a trademark of Tyndale House Publishers, Inc.

The Marriage You've Always Dreamed Of

Published in association with the literary agency of Alive Communications, Inc., 7680 Goddard Street, Suite 200, Colorado Springs, CO 80920.

Some of the names and details in the illustrations used in this book have been changed to protect the privacy of the people who shared their stories.

Designed by Dean H. Renninger

Edited by Lynn Vanderzalm

Library of Congress Cataloging-in-Publication Data

Smalley, Greg.
   The marriage you've always dreamed of / Greg Smalley.
     p. cm.
   Includes bibliographical references.
   ISBN 0-8423-5528-6 (sc)
   1. Spouses—Religious life. 2. Marriage—Religious aspects—Christianity. I. Title.
   BV4596.M3S635 2005
   248.8′44—dc22   2003019280

Printed in the United States of America

10 09 08 07 06 05 04
8   7   6   5   4   3   2   1

To my wife, Erin.

*You have loved me, sacrificed for me,
and inspired me in more ways than
I can express as we journey toward
our Promised Land.*

I love you.

To my friend and colleague Bob Paul.

*Thank you for your vision for and leadership
of the marriage intensive*^{SM} *programs. God has truly gifted
you with amazing talents and insights for strengthening marriage.*

Contents

Acknowledgments

THIS BOOK could not have been developed and written without the extraordinary involvement and help of many people. First, I'd like to thank my wife for her willingness to openly reveal our relationship—our failures and our successes. Also, I'd like to recognize the incredible team at the Smalley Marriage Institute. God has truly blessed me with a wonderful team of men and women who are dedicated to creating a marriage revival throughout the world.

I wish to thank the following people for their collaborative involvement in this project:

My dad, Gary, and brother, Michael, for their friendship and insistence that this book be written.

Bob Paul for developing the marriage intensive^{SM} programs and for the remarkable message and content he has developed for couples.

Dr. Scott Sticksel for his investment in my life, both personally and professionally, and for his insights and wisdom into the development of this book.

Dr. Peter Larson, Dr. Bob Burbee, and Dr. Shawn Stover for their amazing insight captured throughout the pages of this book.

Mark Pyatt, for his friendship and encouragement.

Vicki Wrosch, my assistant, for her hard work and dedication.

Steve Halliday, an exceptionally gifted writer, for being my collaborating writer. Steve captured my heart and vision for marriage and made the Promised Land book come to life.

Greg Johnson and Lee Hough, my agents, for their persistence and encouragement during the writing process.

Lynn Vanderzalm, my editor, for her skills, encouragement, and commitment to excellence.

Ron Beers, Ken Petersen, and Jon Farrar of Tyndale House for their partnership with me and the Smalley Marriage Institute.

And, finally, to the Tyndale House team who has engaged in copyediting, internal design and layout, cover design, and the myriad of details required to bring a book to press.

I thank you all.

Greg Smalley

MEET THE DOC

THE WISEST PATIENTS always do a little investigating before they entrust their physical well-being to the care of a new doctor. They want to know something about this person—details about his or her educational background, work experience, style of practice, philosophy of medicine. They want some assurance that they've come to the right place.

I think those who seek help on how to nurse a sick marriage back to health (or guidance on how to strengthen a basically sound one) ought to have the same concern. They should know a little about the one to whom they come for counsel—*especially* if that doctor claims to help equip his patients to fulfill their dreams for marital happiness in something he calls "Promised Land marriage."

Therefore, before we begin our journey toward a satisfying, healthy marriage, allow me to introduce myself. Permit me to describe a little of my own personal journey so you can feel comfortable with the guide and confident that he is the right one.

FOOLISH BOY

I grew up in the home of Dr. Gary and Norma Smalley, and as their son, I thought that I had this business of marriage all figured out.[1] So when I married Erin in 1992, a year into my master's degree program in counseling psychology at Denver Seminary, I thought my biggest struggles lay behind me.

Foolish kid!

Consider just one example. In our second year of marriage, Erin and I got into a huge argument early one morning. At the time we were living in Denver Seminary's on-campus apartments and as yet didn't realize just how thin those walls were. Our disagreement made her late for work, so right before she slammed the door on her way out, she offered one final, belittling comment.

It really ticked me off, not only that she got in the last word, but also that we hadn't resolved the issue. And I wanted to do something to draw attention to my displeasure.

We used to stuff our dirty clothes into a gigantic mesh bag, then drop the bag, bombardier style, to the laundry room three stories directly below. I had planned to do the laundry that day, so as I noticed the enormous bag sitting on the floor, a spectacularly unwise plan began to form in my fevered brain. I decided to make my point by dropping our clothes as near as possible to Erin as she walked to her car. I didn't want to hit her, just to startle her. Then I'd pretend, "Oh, I'm sorry. I was just dropping the laundry."

A stupid plan? Of course. But remember, I had only seconds to think it through. As I saw my wife angrily rushing down the stairs and hurtling toward her car, I impulsively grabbed the bag, carefully gauged her speed, and let it go.

Unfortunately, my dumb bomb clipped her. It didn't crush her neck or anything nearly so disastrous, but it did launch her off her feet and knock her to the ground. As she lay sprawled out on the turf, she looked up—and saw me still staring out the window.

At that instant it dawned on me: *I'm in big trouble.*

Even though I knew my wife had run track in college, I never fully realized how fast she could climb stairs. I had only seconds to decide what to do. Erin's tough, and I didn't know whether she would pummel me or sling me out the window to join our laundry. I hastily retreated into our apartment and quickly turned the lock. Seconds later I heard her banging furiously on the door. I slinked back against the wall, careful not to make a sound, madly hoping that she might think I had left. I knew only one thing: whatever happened, I was *not* about to open that door.

Our worried neighbors heard the commotion and started streaming out of their apartments—and their curiosity saved me. Unnerved by all the watching eyes, Erin bounded down the stairs and drove off in a cloud of dust.

By the time she returned home that night, I had neatly folded all of the laundry and piled it in the living room so she would know I had done everything. I also strategically positioned four or five bouquets of flowers around our apartment.

We managed to smooth things over that evening, and I apologized for my angry behavior. Erin and I have grown since then, but it wasn't until we began to employ some of the skills and techniques described in this book that we learned how to use conflict as a doorway to greater intimacy.

FURTHER INSTRUCTION

I had enrolled at Denver Seminary to earn a degree in marriage and family counseling, and we stayed on for a third year just to learn from Dr. Gary Oliver, a marriage expert whom I deeply respect.

After leaving Denver Seminary, I decided to get a doctorate. I applied to and was accepted by Rosemead School of Psychology at Biola University in Los Angeles, where I specialized in marriage and family issues. There I read innumerable books and completed exhaustive coursework, all in an effort to try to understand how I could best help couples.

And I grew increasingly frustrated.

The more I read and studied, the less confidence I felt. So many theories and ideas competed for my attention. Which ones actually *worked*? And how did all of this effectively come together?

When I finished at Rosemead, Erin and I returned home to

Branson, Missouri, and there I continued my quest for understanding. What did I really believe about marriage? And how could I help married couples to pursue their dreams and get the most out of their relationships?

Doctoral grads who want a license to practice in the state of Missouri must complete a postdoctoral residency, which requires a specialization. My choice to specialize in marriage therapy meant further marriage counseling, reading, and research. Yet the more I read, the more frustrated I became.

During that period I worked at the Smalley Relationship Center and personally counseled about twenty couples each week. My efforts appeared to be helping a few of them, but everything seemed to be so hit or miss. I just couldn't put together a complete framework. I couldn't say, "Here's what you need to do to make your marriage stronger. This is why you need to do these things. And when you are done, this is what your marriage will look like." So I continued my quest—asking all of the experts, reading, praying.

And early in the morning on two separate occasions, I believe I heard from the greatest Expert of all. God spoke to me in two vivid dreams that continue to inspire and shape my ministry. I'll tell you more about them later, but for now, it's enough to say that the first dream provided the general outline for this book, while the second supplied the motivation to do something about it.

THE IDEA SHARPENS

As I meditated on and developed the ideas in this book, eventually I began to put them into practice. Under the leadership of Bob Paul and with the help of a team of talented colleagues, we started to offer two- and four-day "marriage intensives," in which couples on the brink of divorce received concentrated help with their relationships.

One day a few summers ago a man who sits on the board of the Smalley Relationship Center approached me and said, "Greg,

I really need to talk to you about something. I can't tell you what to do, but God has laid it on my heart to say something to you. I believe he's saying that you're supposed to help lead a marriage revival."

"*What?*" I asked, dumbfounded.

"I don't know," he replied, shaking his head. "But that's what's on my heart. I just wanted you to know, for what it's worth, what I feel God is leading me to say to you."

I made no reply. What could I say? But I thought, *Well, okay. Whatever.*

A couple of weeks later, two business consultants came to Branson to help our board decide a future course for the Smalley Relationship Center. After meeting with the staff for a full day, the consultants returned the next morning and said to me privately, "We need to meet with you."

When we were alone, both men said to me, "We spent some time praying last night, and then this morning we spent some quiet time alone. As we were driving over to this meeting, we started talking. God has laid it on our hearts to tell you that you're supposed to help lead a marriage revival."

"*What?*" I almost shouted.

"We know this is unusual," they said, assuring me that they had arrived at the idea separately, without coordinated efforts. "But we both feel it. And we both thought we should tell you."

"Wow," I whispered. "A couple of weeks ago someone else said the very same thing to me."

The whole idea made me very uneasy.

For the next several days, I kept asking God, "Lord, are you trying to tell me something? Is this for real? Are *people* saying this, or are *you* saying this?" I didn't know for sure, and neither did my wife.

A few days later, while helping to brainstorm about another project, a godly man unconnected to any of this said to me, "Hey, Greg, I want to meet with you before you leave."

When we found a private spot, he cleared his voice and said, "Listen, we've been talking about marriage for the past several days. And you know what? I believe you're supposed to do something. I feel a marriage revival is supposed to take place, and you're supposed to help lead it."

I cut him off. "All right, who have you been talking to?" I demanded.

He looked genuinely surprised. "What do you mean?" he asked.

"Tell me that you've been talking to people," I said.

"I don't know where this is coming from," he replied evenly, "but I believe that's what I'm supposed to tell you."

His words shook me, and I thought, *All right, not one of these people knows the others. No one seems to be plotting anything. Could this really be God?*

Shortly after that encounter I had the second dream, which I'll describe in the next chapter. And finally I admitted what I already knew: *All right, God. It appears as if you're speaking to me. You seem to be saying that I'm supposed to help lead something. Still, I don't understand. It's way too intimidating.*

And at last, on my knees, I said to the Lord, "All right. I submit."

After I returned home, I said to my wife, "I think God is truly calling me to something unique. He wants a marriage revival, and to whatever degree and in whatever way he sees fit, he wants me to be a part of it. So that's what I have to do. If I can stay here in Branson and do it, great. But if he wants me somewhere else, he'll reveal that. Let's just keep praying."

A MOVEMENT TO COVER THE GLOBE

God has continued to lead since then in astonishing ways. My colleagues and I established the Smalley Marriage Institute, where a sharp team of professionals helps at-risk couples who come for the marriage intensives. We can hardly keep up!

Today we find ourselves working with some of the world's top experts on marriage and family issues. We regularly draw on the expertise of bright university professors around the country—all because we're deeply committed to helping ignite a marriage revival, a Spirit-filled movement that God wants to cover the globe.

Why do I tell you the story of my journey? First, it's always exciting to share how God works in our lives. Second, I want you to see that God is behind the beginnings of this marriage revival. Third, I suspect that many of you share my concern for marriages. You may have friends or family members whose marriages are stuck, falling apart, or worse, have already disintegrated. Maybe the marriage falling apart is your own.

The material in this book will give you not only hope but also some significant direction, perspectives, and tools that you can use in your own marriage.

I believe with all of my heart that God wants a marriage revival to rock this country. And I'm certain that he wants your dreams for your own marriage to blossom and grow in the Promised Land.

CHAPTER 1

MARRIAGE 911

Give honor to marriage, and remain
faithful to one another in marriage.

HEBREWS 13:4

NOT LONG AGO I took my family on a vacation to Florida. One evening my two young daughters and I were building a sand castle on a beautiful, powdery white beach. As we worked, I noticed a young boy, about nine years old, circling our growing fortress. He stayed about ten or fifteen yards away from us as he tossed a football to himself. No one seemed to be with him.

Eventually I asked the boy to throw me the ball. We played catch for about five minutes, and then I turned to the girls and asked if we should invite the boy to build with us.

"Sure!" they said.

"Hey, son," I asked, "would you like to help us?"

"Oh, yeah!" he replied enthusiastically.

We all sat in the sand to continue our construction project. Soon I asked the boy, "What's your name?"

"Zachary," he said with pride.

"Nice to meet you, Zachary," I replied. I then introduced my family.

"What are you doing out here?" I asked. "I haven't seen you with anybody."

"Well, I've been at my dad's house," he explained. "Now I'm here at my mom's house."

Immediately I assumed his parents had divorced, but to avoid presuming anything, I said, "Really? So your dad lives somewhere else?"

"Yeah, he lives in Alabama," Zachary replied. "And now I'm here with my mom in Florida."

"Really," I answered. "And what does that mean, Zachary?"

I'll never forget his answer. This nine-year-old boy momentarily took his sandy hands away from the castle, looked up with fear in his eyes, and said in a wavering voice, "I'm not sure, but my mom says it means that I'm now the man of the house."

A feeling of utter sadness washed over me. It bothered me that a nine-year-old boy thought he had to be the "man of the house." This is the job of a father, not of a young boy. I saw the panic in his eyes that he had to do something beyond his years—that he had to grow up too quickly. But do you know what really broke my heart? He longed for his daddy. Nothing can ever replace a father in a child's life—especially the daily interaction. This is where a young boy learns how to be a man. Zachary learned that a dad quit and left him home alone to fend for himself.

Zachary's story breaks my heart. But do you know the saddest thing of all? Millions of Zacharys live all around this country. Untold numbers of hurting little boys and girls grow up in broken homes, forced to accept adult responsibilities long before they're ready. You probably know some of these children. And they're frightened.

Behind every child stung by divorce stand two people who lost their dream of a lifelong, satisfying marriage. Many of them are frightened, too. They often feel sad, lost, and confused.

THE NEED FOR A MARRIAGE REVIVAL

It shouldn't take a sad story like Zachary's to make us realize that America urgently needs a marriage revival. Did you know that

- every day 2,700 children will watch their parents either separate or divorce?[1]
- under current trends in the United States, younger people who marry for the first time face a 40–50 percent chance of divorce?[2]
- second marriages fail at a rate about 10 percent higher than the rate of failed first marriages?[3]
- many first marriages end in divorce in the first three to five years? (In 2000, for example, among women aged 25 to 29 whose first marriages ended in divorce, the median length of marriage was 3.4 years.)[4]
- fewer than half of the marriages that avoid divorce can be described as truly happy?[5]
- marital distress puts both adults and children at increased risk for mental and physical problems? (Common maladies include increased incidence of illness, decreased work productivity—especially for men, suicide, violence, homicide, significant suppression of the immune system, mortality from disease, and increased rates of automobile accidents.)[6]

The people these statistics represent are our neighbors, our family members, our friends, our coworkers. Just look around. This nation urgently needs a marriage revival. The welfare and happiness of countless couples—and let's not forget the millions of little Zacharys—depend on it.

Yet all revivals, of whatever type and wherever they occur, start small. The marriage revival that we need so badly will begin only when individual couples consciously choose to do the hard work necessary to avoid the pain of divorce and instead make their dreams come true by entering into the satisfaction and joy of a Promised Land marriage.

It's this vision that makes me passionate about helping couples to resolve their marital problems. I have dedicated my life to equipping couples to understand, find, and experience God's best for their marriages. But it took two dreams—literal ones, mind you—to get me on track.

A DREAM OF FREEDOM

About two o'clock one morning, I sat bolt upright in bed after experiencing one of the most vivid dreams of my life. The images not only captivated me but also helped me put together some pieces of a difficult puzzle that had confounded me for a long time.

In my dream I stared as the descendants of the Old Testament patriarch Abraham enjoyed "the good life" in Goshen. I watched as God freed the children of Israel from Egyptian slavery. I observed as the ancient Hebrews struggled and learned in the wilderness. I witnessed their supernatural triumph at Jericho. And finally I saw them take possession of the Promised Land under the able leadership of Joshua.

Yet somehow I knew that this vivid dream served as far more than a historical replay; I understood that these ancient Israelites represented *contemporary* married couples. And I knew that what happened to God's chosen people in biblical history could happen to husbands and wives *right now*.

"Whoa!" I murmured the moment I opened my eyes. I sprang out of bed, turned on the computer, and started typing. Here's the artwork for the idea that came to me that morning. It still serves as the framework for my understanding about how best to help couples leave the "slavery" of marital hurts and disappointments in order to enter the Promised Land—their dream relationship, all that God meant marriage to be.

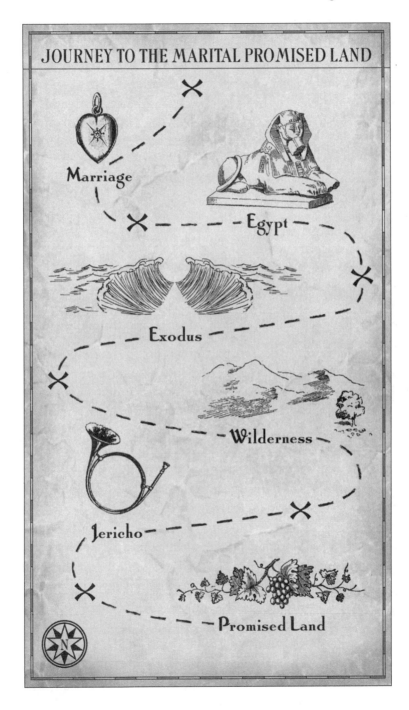

JOURNEY TO THE MARITAL PROMISED LAND

Marriage

Egypt

Exodus

Wilderness

Jericho

Promised Land

We'll unpack this map as we make our way through the book, but for now it's enough to grasp the general idea. The biblical story of Israel's flight from being stuck in Egypt to a new life in God's Promised Land provides a model with the power to point modern marriages to health, courage, and renewed strength. I could never have asked God for such an insightful dream!

And then he gave me a second one.

TASTE THE DUST

Like nearly everyone else in the country on September 11, 2001, I sat glued in front of my television set, watching in horror as the World Trade Center towers disintegrated into a pile of rubble. I could hardly believe that terrorists could stage such a hideous attack, let alone comprehend the vast number of deaths they could inflict so quickly. The tragedy rattled me to the core.

The following month I traveled to Pasadena, California, for a seminar. And for the second time in my life, an impossibly vivid dream awakened me in the wee hours of the morning.

In my dream, I saw the World Trade Center towers still standing, looking down on the rest of the New York skyline. I felt helpless as two hijacked planes once more smashed into a pair of defenseless targets. And I felt weak as I watched both towers crumble into dust.

This dream felt so real that I could taste the dust and smell the smoke. It felt as if I were really *there*.

I quickly realized that, like my previous dream about the ancient Israelites fleeing Egypt, this dream was symbolic: the collapsing towers represented a husband and a wife. In the shadow of their catastrophic fall stood dazed children, wounded families, and crippled communities, all bleeding profusely from the catastrophe of divorce.

In my dream, I was driving a vintage M*A*S*H ambulance. With me rode a team of men and women whose faces I couldn't see but who nevertheless made up a crucial part of the team. On one side of the ambulance, as clear as day, I saw some words stenciled in classic M*A*S*H style: **MARRIAGE 911.**

And then I woke up.

A flood of emotions swept over me. Right there in the hotel room, I broke down and sobbed. Despite my mixed feelings, I got out of bed, booted up the computer, and started writing. I recorded my whole dream. When I finished, I logged on to the Internet and discovered that no one yet owned the rights to the name "Marriage 911." So I grabbed it.

And in those emotion-filled, early morning hours, I knew God had set my agenda for the foreseeable future.

WHY THIS BOOK?

Why have I written this book? To offer help and encouragement to searching husbands and wives? Surely. To create a practical tool that God might use in a marriage revival? That would be terrific. But that is not my core reason.

A deeply personal motive drives me to publish this book. I'm writing for the Zacharys who live all around us. I can never forget that poignant moment on the beach and the desperate longing that I saw deep in Zachary's eyes. I know that those same dejected eyes peer out from millions of little boys and girls all over the country. And I know that behind every Zachary stands a distressed couple, a husband and wife who wanted desperately to make their marriage work but couldn't find the way. They had a dream that died in a puff of smoke and a cloud of dust. The eyes of these couples haunt me.

I write this book for them.

I've dedicated my professional life to helping couples not only make sense of their marriages but also enjoy them in a way they never thought possible. I want them, in other words, to achieve the marriage they've always dreamed of.

What are your dreams for your marriage? What were your dreams on your wedding day? Like some people, you may have had totally unrealistic expectations for your marriage: "I just know that we'll agree on everything and never, ever get into a fight." "I can't wait to get married so I'll never feel alone again." Some dreams have more in common with never-never-land fantasies than with real marriage. Dreams like these tend to die so quickly that most don't even get a decent burial. Unfortunately, this can lead us to believe that *all* our dreams for marriage are nothing but fantasies. Yet that's simply not true.

The Bible reveals several of God's dreams for marriage: close companionship and compatibility; emotional, physical, and spiritual intimacy; homes overflowing with honor, order, respect, and love (see Genesis 2:18, 24; Proverbs 5:15-19; Ephesians 5:21-31; Colossians 3:19; Titus 2:4; Hebrews 13:4; 1 Peter 3:7.) Since these dreams are God's dreams, they're anything but fantasies. They really can come true in your marriage. Beautiful dreams like these, and many more, have a wonderful way of taking root and blossoming in the relationships of husbands and wives committed to journeying together toward a Promised Land marriage. More than anything, that's what I want for you, with all my heart.

We at the Smalley Marriage Institute want to help couples fulfill these God-given dreams. Our goal, as we say on our Web site, is "building, restoring, and renewing the promise of a great marriage."[7] When a husband and wife leave from their experience, they return home equipped with a clear plan and direction for how to achieve their greatest dreams for their marriage.

In an effort to make these dreams come true, we've created, under the leadership of Bob Paul, two- and four-day "marriage intensives" in which couples come to the Institute for concentrated relationship help. We've been tracking the performance of these sessions for the past few years and are delighted to report that they consistently enjoy more than *90 percent* success—that is, less than 10 percent of the couples who complete the program end up filing for divorce, and those who stay together report a significant improvement in their level of marriage satisfaction.

When my dad heard about the phenomenal success we've enjoyed in this program, he wanted to see for himself. So a short while ago he helped lead an intensive. Subsequently I overheard him tell a friend, "I was shocked to see what they're doing. These couples fly in from everywhere and often come in separated from each other, hurt and hostile, having suffered through affairs or any number of horrible things. These husbands and wives don't even know each other when they show up—but at the end of the four days, they leave appearing to be lifetime friends. They return home holding hands."

The insights these hurting couples gain from an intensive, along with the relationship tools they take home with them, make a huge difference in their marriages. But marriages, of course, aren't the only kind of relationships. Over time I began to suspect that the same problems and dilemmas that plague marriages also severely injure relationships of all types—and my colleagues agreed. So I teamed up with "The Relationship Revolution" team—my dad; my brother, Michael; and my colleague Bob Paul—to write *The DNA of Relationships,* a book that shows how we can strengthen healthy relationships and restore hurting ones, whether those relationships get played out at home, at school, at work, in church, in neighborhoods or anywhere else. It develops a comprehensive blueprint for constructing healthy relationships of any kind: friendships, parent-child, sibling, employer-employee, neighbor, whatever.

What is the DNA of relationships? It is simply the genetic relationship code with which we were created. It's our relational hardwiring. The relationship DNA code is made up of three simple yet profound strands:

1. *We are made for relationships.* God hardwired us for relationships. We are made for three kinds of relationships: with others, with ourselves, and with God.
2. *We are made with the capacity to choose.* Too often when relationships go sour, we protest, "But I had no choice!" It's a lie, almost always. We *do* have a choice. Even the choice not to choose is a choice.
3. *We are made to take responsibility for ourselves.* While it's tempting to blame others when relationships don't

work out, we must learn to take personal responsibility. We can take steps to strengthen relationships.

Because my primary focus remains solidly on marriage, *The Marriage You've Always Dreamed Of* takes many of the DNA principles and explores how they work specifically in marriage. This book brings you the benefits enjoyed by the couples—many in serious relationship distress—who leave our marriage intensives hand in hand. What happens in those intensives can also happen wherever you live. And it can start *today*.

JOIN ME! SEE CHANGES!

Are you ready for a marriage revival? More to the point, are you ready to revive your own marriage? Are you ready to build the marriage of your dreams? If so, I invite you to join me.

I'm thrilled at what God is doing through our work at the Smalley Marriage Institute and pleased that I have some small place in it. I'm delighted that our marriage intensives have racked up a 90 percent success rate—but I'm no longer surprised by it. In one sense, *of course* we're going to have 90 percent success. Why? Because this marriage revival is God's idea.

I believe with all of my heart that God wants a marriage revival to spread over the whole world. And I'm certain that he wants your own marriage to blossom and grow in the Promised Land.

Do you want that, too? Then join us. Read this book. Try out the principles in your marriage. Share hope with the couples around you. Be part of God's work to strengthen marriages all around the world.

So, where do we start? We start where ancient Israel started: in the giddy days of a fresh beginning.

1

Living Well in Goshen

CHAPTER 2

WHEN THE GOOD TIMES ROLL

Pharaoh said to Joseph, "Now that your family has joined you here, choose any place you like for them to live. Give them the best land of Egypt—the land of Goshen will be fine." . . . So the people of Israel settled in the land of Goshen in Egypt. And before long, they began to prosper there, and their population grew rapidly.

GENESIS 47:5-6, 27

THE STORY OF the Promised Land journey in the Bible begins when the family of Jacob moved to Goshen. It was a great time for them. They lived in peace and stability. Their families grew. Their flocks multiplied.

The early months and years of marriage can be like that. Life is good, and you take things in stride.

Several months before Erin and I got married, I invited her to help me move from Phoenix, Arizona, to Denver, Colorado. I wanted her to see where she would be living the following year. Since we hoped to cover those 1,200 miles in a single day, we planned to meet at my parents' house at about five o'clock in the morning and drive until we reached Denver.

By the time my lovely fiancée arrived, I had loaded up a U-Haul truck (equipped with a stick shift, which I'd never driven) and hitched my car to the towing bar behind the trailer. Erin and I said good-bye to my family—an emotional time, since I was leaving the area—and excitedly lurched off on our adventure. As I pulled out of the driveway and rumbled down the street, I looked in the side mirror . . . and saw my dad frantically chasing us.

"What do I do?" I asked, rolling my eyes, "He's running after me! And he's a marathon runner. How far will he chase us?"

"Pull over," Erin said compassionately. "I'm sure he just wants to give you one final hug good-bye."

"This is so embarrassing," I complained. "It's time to let me go! Cut the cord already! I'm twenty-two years old, for crying out loud!" Nevertheless, I stopped and rolled down my window, expecting to hear an emotional plea to be careful. That's not what I got.

"Greg, you knucklehead!" he yelled. "Didn't you notice what's still parked in front of my house?"

I looked carefully in the mirror, and sure enough, there sat my car. Somehow, the car must have bounced off the hitch. It turned out that I'd forgotten to insert the safety pin on the trailer ball. "So, that's what that's for!" I exclaimed after making the discovery. Erin thought it "cute" that I didn't think to check the safety pin, and she laughed hysterically.

I backed up the truck, reattached my car, and fastened the safety pin. Unfortunately, my mistake had cost us about forty-five minutes. I figured we could still make Denver by late night—but by four o'clock that afternoon, I already felt bone tired.

"Honey, you have to drive," I said. "I'm really exhausted."

"You have to be kidding," she replied. "There's no *way* I'm driving this big truck!"

I'd hoped for a different response, but I still gave her the benefit of the doubt—after all, I loved her. So with no other options open to me, I declared my need for some "stuff" to keep me awake. I figured that since Erin is a nurse, I spoke to the right person.

"I can solve that real fast," she declared. "Pull into that truck stop."

When I did, she hopped out of the truck, and a few minutes

later she returned to load me up with a bag full of No-Doz tablets, Jolt cola, weight-loss pills—anything with high levels of caffeine.

"Are you sure I can take all of this stuff together?" I asked, a little concerned.

"Sure," she replied, "trust me." Then I heard her mumble under her breath, "At least, I guess it's all right."

I quickly doused my system with wild rivers of caffeine, and the moment it hit, I felt as if I could drive 120,000 miles, not a mere 1,200. I smiled broadly at Erin, leaned over, and shouted, "How far is Canada?" We drove on, laughing and watching the scenery fly by.

But by one o'clock in the morning the caffeine had worn off, and I couldn't drive another mile.

"If we don't find a place to stop immediately," I whined, "I'm going to kill us."

We had nearly reached Colorado Springs, Colorado, and it seemed as good a place as any to stop. But we immediately ran into a big problem. Parents' Weekend at the Air Force Academy had arrived, and every room in every hotel and motel in the city had been taken (now I know how Mary and Joseph must have felt stumbling into Bethlehem). We searched for a frustrating hour before someone suggested, "I guarantee there'll be a room at a certain motel downtown."

Horse stable or not, I thought, here we come!

When we arrived at the U-shaped, rundown motel with an office shack in the middle, I wheeled our truck around the whole complex. By then my exhaustion had nearly given way to delirium.

"I need two rooms," I told the office manager.

"Sorry, I have only one," he answered.

Of course! I thought. Why break precedent now? The rest of the trip has been one disaster after another.

"Does it have two beds?" I asked.

"No, just one."

Oh, all right. I guess I'll sleep on the floor. No big deal. At least we'll have two pillows.

"I'll take it," I replied wearily.

"How many hours would you like the room for?" he asked.

What a bizarre question. Nevertheless, I consulted my watch. It was 2:35 A.M. If we could sleep for five hours, we would still make Denver by nine o'clock in the morning.

"I need the room for five hours," I said.

"Way to *go*, buddy!" he snorted.

Completely oblivious to his meaning, I replied innocently, "Most of the time, I rent a room all night."

The man doubled over with laughter and gave me a high five.

Odd, I thought, as I turned away from the counter.

"This is really a strange place," I told Erin, "but it's our only option. I'll sleep on the floor. Let's call our parents to let them know."

But the phones wouldn't work. The last straw! *Forget it*, I thought, and took my place on the cold, hard floor. The next morning, I woke up stiff from a terrible night's sleep. I hobbled over to the office and handed my keys to the same man who had checked us in the night before. He seemed terribly upset.

"Buddy," I asked, "what's wrong?"

"None of the phones work, and people are yelling at me!" he moaned. "I can't figure out why. This is going to cost me *money!*"

"Tell me about it," I replied. "My fiancée and I tried to call our parents last night to let them know what happened. We didn't want anyone to wonder why we stayed in the same room, so we . . ."

My voice trailed off when it became clear he had zero interest in my story. I left to buy Erin a diet Coke—and noticed a severed cable lying on the ground. *That's weird*, I thought.

As I walked around the complex, every few feet I noticed another severed cable lying on the pavement—until I reached my truck. There, six inches from the front of my vehicle, hung one last cable still in place. And then it hit me: I had clipped all the phone lines when I drove around the facility the night before!

I ran into our room, yelling, "Erin! Get into the truck *now!* We have to get out of here!"

Erin, of course, wondered if I had just robbed the manager. When she heard the real story, she rightly insisted that we stay and face the music. After I tabulated all of the damage, I realized that crummy little room ended up costing me more than a presidential suite.

Still, we laughed all the way from Colorado Springs to Denver. How? Why? Because when you're young and in love and at the front end of your relationship, the whole world seems delightful. Everything tickles your funny bone. That's almost always how it is at the beginning.

GOOD TIMES IN GOSHEN— THE WONDER YEARS

Most couples begin their relationship on a healthy diet of fun times, happy moments, and memorable outings. They're in love, and the world is their oyster. Things could not be better.

Not long ago we asked couples at our monthly marriage seminar to describe the best part of their first year of marriage. Do you remember feeling some of these things back then?

- The newness and excitement (the butterflies) of starting our life together.
- Coming home to a person who cares about what happens to me during the day.
- Moving in together. Having our own apartment, filling up the house with stuff.
- Being able to sleep together and hold one another (a slumber party every night). Sharing our life goals, future plans, and dreams.
- Having a best friend with me all the time.
- Being the center of my spouse's attention. It was just us.

We could pack up and go at any time; things didn't have
to be planned.
- Very poor but happy and on our own.
- Making new traditions and knowing that we were a team
  and tackling problems, situations, and ideas together.
- The optimism that we could overcome anything.
- Learning how to cope with the differences we discovered.

I liken this stage of the relationship to the blissful experience of ancient Israel as described near the end of Genesis. By
that time, Joseph had won the admiration and favor of Pharaoh
and had risen to the second most powerful position in Egypt,
answering only to the king himself. When Pharaoh heard that
Joseph's long-lost brothers had arrived in his kingdom, he told
Joseph, "Tell them to bring your father and all of their families,
and to come here to Egypt to live. Tell them, 'Pharaoh will as-
sign to you the very best territory in the land of Egypt. You will
live off the fat of the land!' . . . For the best of all the land of
Egypt is yours" (Genesis 45:18, 20).

The brothers wisely obeyed the king, and when they returned,
Pharaoh directed them to acquire property in Goshen, "the best
land of Egypt" (Genesis 47:6). The Israelites "began to prosper
there, and their population grew rapidly" (Genesis 47:27). How
could they help but enjoy their privileged new life in a rich and
welcoming land?

The years passed, and as Joseph's father, Jacob, lay near death,
he prophesied over his son: "Joseph is a fruitful tree, a fruitful tree
beside a fountain. His branches reach over the wall. . . . His bow
remained strong, and his arms were strengthened by the Mighty
One of Jacob, the Shepherd, the Rock of Israel. May the God of
your ancestors help you; may the Almighty bless you with the
blessings of the heavens above, blessings of the earth beneath,
and blessings of the breasts and womb" (Genesis 49:22, 24-25).

Now *that's* a blessing. How could things possibly get better?

For a while Joseph and his family lived a dream. They enjoyed life and feasted off of "the fat of the land." They increased

in number and multiplied their joy. Every day the wise among them thanked God for their rich blessings.

Most of us begin our married lives in a similar state of blessedness. We feel like Joseph and his brothers, blessed to overflowing by a gracious God. We revel in our wonderful partner, whom we consider a priceless gift sent from heaven to bring us satisfaction and joy. We feel thoroughly delighted in the Goshen stage of marriage—and why not? It's *good* to live in Goshen!

HIGHEST LEVEL OF SATISFACTION

The vast majority of couples start off their married lives feeling as if they've settled down in Goshen. They're highly idealistic, with heads crammed full of romantic notions. Who gets married hoping to get a divorce?

A fair amount of research has been done to understand this joyful state of affairs. Husbands and wives often enjoy their highest level of relationship satisfaction from the engagement period through the first year of marriage. In fact, the biggest drop in marital satisfaction occurs during or after that first year. Why? Disillusionment sets in, primarily because of unmet expectations. But before the disillusionment hits, most couples live in marital bliss.

In this Goshen stage, you interpret almost everything your spouse says or does in a positive light. He or she can do no wrong. You view even unpleasant behavior through a positive lens, producing a "perfect" image that emphasizes a spouse's appealing features and conceals the undesirable ones. In a sense, this perspective becomes "closed," so that almost no unpleasant elements can enter the picture. No wonder marriage satisfaction reaches a high point during these early months!

Fortunately for Erin and me, we spent many of the early days of our marriage in Goshen. I'll bet you didn't know that Yellowstone National Park is actually in Goshen, did you? We made that happy discovery on a memorable camping trip—memorable primarily because I made no plans ahead of time.

As we drove through the park, we encountered heavy, bumper-to-bumper traffic. The stop-and-go driving got so bad that Erin started feeling nauseated. Since I worried that the stench of her vomit would make *me* sick and since we had come in my pickup, I would not let her lean out the window to throw up. Instead, I stopped the car and forced her to get out and hike into the woods.

But the sweet air of Goshen prevailed!

By late afternoon we had finally cleared most of the traffic. Since I had made no reservations, however, we couldn't find a camping spot. We drove and drove until I finally got so frustrated that I pulled off the road and ventured deep into the woods—despite my wife's protests. "It's illegal!" she insisted. Erin was sure she had seen a series of warning signs: Beware of Bears. Do Not Feed the Bears. Store Your Food!

Confident in my own plan, I didn't believe a word she said.

We finally found what looked like a suitable spot, and after we set up our tent, we took out our food to prepare for dinner. But since we both felt exhausted after the long trip, we decided to take a quick nap. We laid out a big blanket and settled into the romantic, peaceful setting. Everything seemed perfect. I quickly floated off into a dreamy semiconsciousness. I became disoriented when I heard a rustling noise about ten feet from our blanket. Was that a black, furry head popping up out of the bushes?

At that moment, no more than two inches from my ear, my wife screamed, *"Bear!"*

I'm not sure who felt more startled, me or the bear. We both jumped about three feet into the air. The bear instantly ran up a tree, and I instantly jumped into the truck and locked the doors. Once I reached the safety of my truck, everything seemed fine—until I noticed that I had locked Erin out. My decision didn't go over too well, but since we still resided in Goshen, the icicles soon melted.

The bear remained in the tree for quite some time. I finally got up the nerve to take pictures of this poor, frightened creature stranded so high in the branches. I would have taken more photos, but soon the bushes started rustling again. And before whatever else was moving in there could make an appearance, Erin and I fled.

By that time darkness had fallen. We felt hungry and tired and, of course, we had no camping site. We finally drove out of the park to try our luck in the next town. Since we (again) failed to call ahead, we encountered nothing but a series of No Vacancy signs. At last we located a tiny motel in the middle of nowhere. We ended up sharing the spot with a group of Hell's Angels who apparently had the same idea (or problem). So Erin and I spent our first camping trip together—not bedding down in the beautiful Yellowstone National Park, but lounging in a dingy motel.

Not to break precedent, I attempted to cook our food inside on a portable propane stove—a definite no-no. Even so, it might have worked had it not been for the smoke alarm I set off trying to roast our marshmallows.

It was one of my first big disasters as a newlywed, a huge headache—and yet we still laughed about it. This black cloud had no silver lining, but it had one the color of burnt marshmallows. And that cloud rained on us, not drops of discord, but showers of grace. Why? Because in the Goshen stage of marriage, even stupid screwups can transform themselves into endearing episodes.

(And boy, am I glad!)

THE AMAZING BENEFITS OF MARRIAGE

Couples in the Goshen stage may not consciously realize it— they're too busy enjoying each other—but their union gives them enormous benefits and special advantages over their unmarried counterparts.

Studies conducted all over the world, involving both genders and representing a wide variety of socioeconomic circumstances and ethnicities, prove that married people tend to be healthier, live longer, have more wealth and economic assets, and enjoy more satisfying sexual relationships than single or cohabitating individuals. A marvelous book titled *The Case for Marriage* lays out an impressive argument for the advantages of marriage. Consider a few of the many benefits offered by matrimony:

- Suffering from any psychiatric disorder over a lifetime is significantly lower for those in a legal marriage.[1]
- Married men earn more, work more, and attend church more often. They also frequent bars and taverns less.[2]
- A survey of 18,000 adults in seventeen industrialized nations found that married persons have a significantly higher level of happiness than unmarried adults, even after controlling for health and financial status, which are also linked to marriage.[3]
- Married men and women in all age groups are less likely to be limited in activity (a general health indicator) due to illness than single, separated, divorced, or widowed individuals.[4]
- The absence of marriage is a greater factor in explaining crime rates and poverty than is race.[5]
- One random sample of more than 8,600 adults revealed that married persons suffer less from loneliness (defined as the "absence of satisfying social relationships") than do others. The study found that only 4.6 percent of married individuals felt lonely, opposed to 14.5 percent of never-married individuals, 20.4 percent of divorced individuals, 20.6 percent of those widowed, and 30 percent of individuals who were separated.[6]

Experts also have demonstrated the positive effects of marriage on children by comparing the lives of sons and daughters who live in divorced or single-parent homes with the lives of children whose parents have remained married. In general, children reared in two-parent families do better emotionally and academically than those from single-parent homes.[7] And beyond that:

- Divorce increases the incidence of health problems in children by 50 percent.[8]
- Children from disrupted marriages suffer a 20 to 30 percent greater rate of injury than other children.[9]
- Children living with formerly married mothers had a 50 percent greater risk of having asthma.[10]
- Children living with never-married mothers have an increased risk of speech defects.[11]
- Children reported to have received professional help for emotional or behavior problems varied from 2.7 percent for children living with both biological parents to 8.8 percent for children living with formerly married mothers. For children living with never-married mothers or with mothers and stepfathers, the respective proportions were 4.4 percent and 6.6 percent.[12]

Author and marriage expert Maggie Gallagher sums up the situation like this: "A wide body of social science literature confirms that marriage is a powerful protector of public health. Children raised by their own two married parents live longer, have fewer illnesses and accidents, and enjoy better health than children raised outside of intact marriages. Both men and women who get and stay married enjoy similar powerful health advantages: they live longer, enjoy better health, manage chronic illness better, are less likely to require extensive (and expensive) hospitalization and nursing home care, and become disabled less often than do people who are single or divorced."[13]

Of course, you can have a great time in marriage without even realizing the enormous benefits it brings. But imagine how much *more* thrilling marriage can be when you consciously appreciate its tangible benefits.

WHY MARRIAGES SUCCEED . . .
"AND THE SURVEY SAYS"

Why do some marriages thrive and others end in disaster? As you can imagine, much has been written about why marriages succeed or fail. Many experts have described how successful couples recreate Goshen in their relationship. Interestingly enough, most of the research reveals that a lasting marriage results from a couple's ability to resolve the conflicts inevitable in any relationship. Let's look at some of the specific reasons why marriages succeed:

- Couples, and especially husbands, who stay married expressed more spontaneous fondness and admiration for their spouses. Marriage expert Dr. John Gottman found that husbands and wives in stable marriages expressed five times as much positive feeling and interaction toward one another than did others.

PROMISED LAND TIP
Learn to express five times more positive feelings—affection, admiration, affirmation—than negative feelings.

Moreover, couples who succeed turn toward each other in the everyday aspects of life more than they turn away from one another. And what is the secret of "turning toward"? Gottman says it's requited interest, excitement, and affection, as well as requited irritability.[14]

- Successful couples use humor, affection, and interest five times as much in solving their problems as unsuccessful couples do.[15]
- Men who did more housework and participated more in childcare had better sex lives and happier marriages than others.[16] (Men, I hope you're paying attention!)

Especially interesting are the findings of marriage and family experts David Olson and Amy Sigg. They surveyed 5,153 happy couples and 5,127 unhappy couples and discovered that, compared to unhappy couples, happy couples stated the following:

- I am very satisfied with how we talk to each other.
- We are creative in how we handle our differences.
- We feel very close to each other.
- When discussing problems, my partner understands my opinions and ideas.
- I am completely satisfied with the amount of affection from my partner.
- We have a good balance of leisure time spent together and separately.
- My partner's friends or family rarely interfere with our relationship.
- We agree on how to spend money.
- I am satisfied with how we express spiritual values and beliefs.[17]

In a landmark twenty-five-year research project that studied 14,000 families around the world, Dr. Nick Stinnett, another marriage expert, found that strong families have at least six major things in common:

1. *Commitment:* trust, honesty, dependability, faithfulness
2. *Appreciation and affection:* caring for each other, friendship, respect for individuality, and playfulness and humor
3. *Positive communication:* sharing feelings, giving compliments, avoiding blame, being able to compromise, agreeing to disagree
4. *Time together:* quality time in great quantity (good things take time), enjoying each other's company, simple good times, and sharing fun times
5. *Spiritual well-being:* faith, compassion, shared ethical values, oneness with humankind
6. *Ability to cope with stress:* adaptability, growing through crises together, openness to change, resilience[18]

Let's turn our attention toward two of the most important reasons why marriages succeed.

Spending Time Together

In the excellent book *The Seven Principles for Making Marriage Work*, John Gottman and Nan Silver suggest that successful marriages require that husbands and wives know one another and periodically update their knowledge. Gottman and Silver found that husbands who developed a "map" of their wives' worlds, who made it their business to know their wives' psychological world, wound up in the 33 percent whose marital satisfaction remained high when a couple made the transition to parenthood.[19]

In a survey of my own, I spent a year polling about 10,000 couples regarding their time before they got married. "If you could give only one piece of advice to not-yet-married couples," I asked, "what would it be?" I wanted to understand the most critical elements of a new relationship.

One answer came through loud and clear: *spend time together*. Time together seems to revolve around two important issues: doing things together and making the relationship a top priority. These couples not only spent a lot of time with one another, they also made one another their top priority. I found many terms repeated: *undivided attention, alone time, putting each other first, personal attention, being with my intended, desiring to be together*. Listen to how some couples talked about spending time together:

- We looked forward to talking and being together.
- We spent hours and hours together.
- We loved the time we had together, just the two of us: romance, adventures together, and communication.
- We remember the thrill of constantly being in close contact.
- We enjoyed getting wrapped up in the actual relationship rather than the wedding.
- We were willing to try things we weren't exactly comfortable with.

Time together can mean lots of things: mutual ministry, sharing common interests, trips, meals, coffee-shop talks, trying new things, beach walks, parties, you name it. The key, according to these 10,000 couples, is to do it *together*.

When Erin and I were planning our wedding, I remained in Denver. Although at the time I didn't consider it a big deal, I now grieve that I didn't get more involved. Don't get me wrong—my bride did a wonderful job. We enjoyed a beautiful wedding ceremony and reception. It's just that I could have incorporated some of my own ideas as well. And to be honest, a couple of things caught me by surprise. One in particular.

During the service I wore a lapel microphone so that my voice could be recorded for our wedding video. We sang some very traditional hymns, and unfortunately I didn't have a single lyric available to me on the platform. So I made up words and sang them so far out of tune that I would have cracked the church's stained glass, had there been any. I figured that if I made it appear as if I knew what to sing, no one would be the wiser. I had a foolproof plan . . . almost.

When Erin and I returned home from our honeymoon, we invited family and friends to look at pictures from our trip and to watch the wedding video. The large crowd "oohed" and "aahed" while the tape played. But as the first hymn played, a strange and frightening noise marred the recording. Frame by frame, the noise grew louder and more obnoxious. The hideous commotion literally started to hurt my ears. Our guests contorted their faces, trying to determine the origin of the mysterious, repulsive sound.

A Bible verse describes my situation at that moment: "Your sin will find you out" (Numbers 32:23). In a flash of recognition, I realized the grotesque noise came from *me*. I tried to slither out of the room, but just as escape seemed possible, someone recognized my "singing." I had been exposed! The news spread like wildfire in a tinderbox forest. In unison, the group howled with laughter (and ridicule). I have yet to live it down.

So what's the moral to this little story of woe? Couples who want to live long in Goshen spend time, and lots of it, with each other. If they don't, they, too, may end up on a crowded couch, with derisive laughter turning their faces an ever-darker hue of red.

Learning about Each Other

It's crucial for husbands and wives to spend time with one another. But should they direct all of this time toward any specified goal? The 10,000 couples we surveyed certainly thought so. Second on their list was "getting to know each other on a deep level."

Happy couples increase their knowledge of one another. If you want to live long in Goshen, you must develop a large fund of knowledge about your partner. You must learn his or her likes, dislikes, personality quirks—everything. Every husband and wife ought to "earn a Ph.D. in each other" during their first year of marriage.

Tellingly, a lack of knowledge about each other led to some of the worst times in the engagement period for many couples. One pair wrote, "The most difficult part of our engagement was learning each other's weaknesses and knowing we would have to deal with them regularly." Another person declared a personal frustration: "I found out late in the engagement that he really didn't like shopping, and I had thought for several years that he loved to shop." If you don't get to deeply know your spouse, you may well discover that differences in your backgrounds and circumstances can wound your marriage.

> **PROMISED LAND TIP**
> Every day spend time earning a Ph.D. in your spouse.

Our 10,000 couples discussed expectations, finances, religion, sex, children, family, holidays, family histories, personal memories, interests, habits, medical records, dreams, needs, beliefs, goals, roles, traditions—in short, anything and everything that helped them to gain a better window into the soul of their spouses. One person advised, "Discuss every decision, every vision, and do those things together. If along the way you find you're uninterested or unwilling to experience these activities together—or at least, if you have no desire to find such an interest—then you are not a match."

Such a growing knowledge base produces confidence and assures both people that they have chosen "the right one." And that makes for a long and happy residency in Goshen!

LIVING BY YOUR VOWS

Married couples who enjoy a significant time in the Goshen stage also share at least one other thing in common: an unyielding commitment to each other. They treat their marriage vows as a sacred covenant. They consider their union a binding agreement before God to stick together, no matter what.

In 1999 the growing Covenant Marriage Movement began with the belief that

> God intends for marriage to be a lifelong covenant relationship between a man and a woman. When a couple shares their wedding vows, they are vowing to God, each other, their families, and their community to remain steadfast in unconditional love, reconciliation, and sexual purity, while purposefully growing in their covenant marriage relationship. God desires to bring wholeness to families through covenant marriage relationships.
>
> God has instilled in the hearts of couples from every walk of life the need to affirm His intent for their marriage. In signing the covenant, couples will be joining thousands of other couples across the nation and around the world in affirming the importance of a covenant marriage relationship. But for you and your spouse, it will be committing yourselves to each other to remain steadfast in the unconditional love God expects of you and provides for you.[20]

I heartily endorse the movement and the vow it has developed, as do such diverse groups as Focus on the Family, the

Assemblies of God, Moody Bible Institute, Promise Keepers, and Lifeway Christian Resources. Why do they all agree that this is an idea whose time has come? For one thing, God himself uses the term *marriage covenant*. In describing a wife, he calls her "your partner, the wife of your marriage covenant" (Malachi 2:14, NIV).

Second, the covenant marriage idea *works*. Couples around the world are embracing this idea as a way to bring God deeper into their marriage. Ministry leaders from the four corners of the globe use covenant marriage as a tool to strengthen marriages and thus strengthen congregations and ultimately the entire Body of Christ.

If you have not already done so, I urge you—as husband and wife, together—to repeat together and sign the following vow. Carefully study the words, making sure that you understand the commitment they reflect. And then put them into practice.

BELIEVING THAT MARRIAGE is a covenant intended by God to be a lifelong, fruitful relationship between a man and a woman, we vow to God, each other, our families, and our community to remain steadfast in unconditional love, reconciliation, and sexual purity, while purposefully growing in our covenant marriage relationship.

_____

(YOUR NAME HERE)

_____

(YOUR NAME HERE)

God's covenant with Abraham to bless his descendants and give them the land of Egypt and eventually the Promised Land brought the ancient Hebrews to Goshen. Similarly, a modern covenant can help husbands and wives to claim their own private Goshens and journey to the Promised Land marriage. All of them can build the marriage of their dreams, the kind of marriage that brings satisfaction and joy.

As I've been hinting, however, no marriage stays in Goshen forever. Things happen, and they tend to move us out of Goshen and into an entirely different land.

> **PROMISED LAND TIP**
> Treat your marriage vows as a sacred covenant by making an unyielding commitment to each other.

WHAT A DIFFERENCE A FEW YEARS MAKE

It took Leonardo da Vinci seven years to complete his masterpiece *The Last Supper*. He used living models for the figures representing Christ and the twelve apostles, and the artist began his work by choosing the model for Jesus.

Hundreds of young men went through a tough screening process for the honor of providing the likeness of Christ. Da Vinci looked for a face and personality that represented innocence and beauty, free of the ugly blemish of sin. After a diligent search lasting many weeks, the artist selected a nineteen-year-old. For six months da Vinci worked on this part of his painting.

The artist continued to work on his masterpiece for the next six years. He carefully selected models for each of the apostles, saving space for the final disciple, Judas Iscariot, the betrayer. For this final figure, the artist searched long and hard for a man with a hard, callous face, pockmarked with the scars of avarice, deceit, and hypocrisy—a face that looked as if it belonged to a man who could betray his best friend. Finally da Vinci heard about a man who fully met his artistic requirements. The scoundrel lay in a prison cell in Rome, awaiting execution for murder.

When the painter arrived in Rome, officials brought the prisoner out of his dark cell and into the light of the sun—a swarthy man with long, shaggy, unkempt hair that covered his cruel face. Instantly da Vinci knew he had found his model, a character in complete moral ruin.

The king permitted the prisoner to be taken to Milan, where for months the convict sat before the artist. When da Vinci completed his painting, he turned to the guards and announced, "I have finished. You may take the prisoner away."

Without warning, the man broke loose from the guards' control and ran up to the artist, shouting, "O, da Vinci, look at me! Do you not know who I am?"

The great artist focused his trained eyes on the ruined figure and once more carefully scrutinized his features. "No," he replied, "I have never seen you in my life until you were brought before me out of the dungeon in Rome."

At those words the prisoner lifted his eyes to heaven and cried out, "O God, have I fallen so low?" Then he turned his face to the painter and said, "Leonardo da Vinci! Look at me again, for I am the same man you painted just seven years ago as the figure of Christ!"[21]

Yes, it's possible. The same man who provides the model for Christ can, just a few years later, look exactly like Judas. And do you want to know something? A similar thing can happen to our marriages. We may start out in Goshen, but many of us wind up somewhere else, all too quickly.

A place that looks an awful lot like slavery.

PART

2

Getting Stuck
in Egypt

CHAPTER 3

DESCENDING INTO MISERY

Then a new king came to the throne of Egypt who knew nothing about Joseph or what he had done. He told his people, "These Israelites are becoming a threat to us because there are so many of them. We must find a way to put an end to this. If we don't and if war breaks out, they will join our enemies and fight against us. Then they will escape from the country." So the Egyptians made the Israelites their slaves and put brutal slave drivers over them, hoping to wear them down under heavy burdens.

EXODUS 1:8-11

LIVING IN A big city can present outsiders with many challenges, not the least among them issues of safety. Erin never felt totally safe in our Los Angeles neighborhood during the years we spent at Rosemead, so we bought an alarm system. Unfortunately, neither of us ever became an expert at using it.

Once when we decided to take a trip out of town, Erin asked a friend to house-sit. The young woman came over one evening to get familiar with her duties, and Erin greeted her warmly. But since I was watching a basketball game that I didn't want to miss, I ignored them.

I heard Erin trying valiantly to explain how the alarm worked, but she struggled to remember the right numbers for an alternate code (she didn't want to give out our permanent code). She called out to me for assistance, but I continued to ignore her. She glared at me (I felt the icicles) and then gave our friend the code she remembered. The young woman practiced the procedure and finally left about nine o'clock.

Erin, still steaming, walked upstairs, all the while giving me the evil eye. In those fleeting moments she successfully communicated her message: "Thanks a lot for all your help."

We lived in a little town house with a downstairs living room and an upstairs bedroom. When I belatedly realized the extent of my wife's wrath, I pursued her upstairs to try to work out the problem. But by then she had begun getting ready for bed and had no desire to reengage; she needed time to cool down. But her silence irritated me, and I said so.

I had stormed off to the bathroom to get myself ready for bed when I heard her say, "I think there's someone at the door."

"Oh, maybe it's what's-her-name," I answered. "Maybe she has some final questions about house-sitting."

"Oh, all right," she replied, recognizing that I had no intention of answering the door. She walked downstairs and a few moments later yelled up at me, "It's the police!"

"Yeah, right," I said, not believing her. After several minutes I called out, "Erin . . . ?" But only silence answered me.

Several minutes later I went downstairs to find the front door wide open, with Erin nowhere in sight. I had taken out my contacts and strained to look past the door, but I could see nothing in the darkness. I moved closer to the door and heard a commanding voice: "Freeze! Don't move! Put your hands up!"

I still couldn't see anything, but the voice made me think that guns had been drawn.

"Erin!" I called out. "Where are you?"

No answer.

The voice continued to yell instructions: "Come down the walkway!"

Assuming that the police had shown up for some reason, I slowly moved down the pavement. When I finally saw Erin, I reached out my arms to embrace her. She ran right up to me, angrier than ever, and started screaming at me.

"I am so *ticked* at you!" she shouted. "You never help me. You ignore me!"

"*What* are you talking about?" I asked, bewildered. "What is the problem?"

"When I asked for your help about the alarm code, you kept watching TV. This is all *your* fault!" she stormed.

I looked around again, dimly saw a phalanx of police officers, and asked, "What is going on?"

"I put in the silent alarm code, thinking it was the right one," Erin explained. "This is all *your* fault! The cops are here because I tripped the silent alarm!"

Until that night, we both loved the silent alarm feature. If a robber pulled a gun on us and told us to turn off our alarm, we could punch in the silent alarm code instead. That's like Code Red, and the police arrive with guns drawn.

Forgetting all about the officers, I started yelling back. "What were you thinking? You *know* the right code. Why are you blaming me?"

We traded accusations for some time until a police officer tapped both of us on the shoulders. "I don't mean to interrupt your discussion here," he said evenly, "but is there anyone in that house that we need to be concerned about? Can you at least tell us *that,* so we can go home? You two can finish arguing out here in the front if you want."

Friends, if an L.A. cop has never rebuked you, you don't know what you're missing.

How had Erin and I gone from blissful days of enjoying each other's company, serving each other, wanting the best for each other, to heated nights of public shouting matches? I'll tell you: we took a trip sadly familiar to married couples the world over. Somewhere along the way we left the green pastures of Goshen and found ourselves groaning under the sharp lash of misery in Egypt.

FALLING INTO MISERY

The Bible doesn't tell us how long the Israelites lived it up on the fat of the land, but sometime after Joseph died, a new Egyptian leader emerged. This man felt threatened by the exploding Hebrew population, and he forced the Israelites into harsh slavery:

> So the Egyptians made the Israelites their slaves and put brutal slave drivers over them, hoping to wear them down under heavy burdens. They forced them to build the cities of Pithom and Rameses as supply centers for the king. But the more the Egyptians oppressed them, the more quickly the Israelites multiplied! The Egyptians soon became alarmed and decided to make their slavery more bitter still. They were ruthless with the Israelites, forcing them to make bricks and mortar and to work long hours in the fields. (Exodus 1:11-14)

The Israelites fell fast, long, and hard. They went from harvesting their own crops on the best of the land to working as slaves in the parched fields of others. Somehow they exchanged blessing for bitterness, happy for hard. And the Bible says, "But the Israelites still groaned beneath their burden of slavery. They cried out for help, and their pleas for deliverance rose up to God" (Exodus 2:23).

Maybe you know the feeling. Perhaps you remember better days in the early years of your marriage, but today you look around at a dull and seemingly lifeless marriage. One moment things seemed to be going great, the next you felt burdened by conflict and distance. What went wrong?

Most marriages run into trouble when husbands and wives make two mistakes: they *stop* doing things that strengthen the relationship, and they *start* doing things that hurt it. Repeated disappointments, arguments, and frustrations lead to conflict, negativity, and dullness. A wife may shift her attitude from admiration to faultfinding; suddenly the husband can do no right. A husband may interpret everything his wife says or does in a negative way; she simply can't win. When our relationships run into persistent problems, we all have a tendency to switch "lenses" and see our spouse in a negative light. And when this happens, the relationship descends into misery.

DON'T STOP DOING THE GOOD THINGS

When I'm wearing my counselor hat and first meet with a couple in trouble, I normally remind the pair of how they started out. Based on phone interviews or questionnaires, I try to clearly identify the specific activities they once enjoyed, the things they did to build up the marriage and make it satisfying. I attempt to jog their memory about how they used to spend time together, how they consciously made an effort to learn more about their spouse. I want them to get a clear picture of what they once did (but stopped doing), so they can do it again. I consider it emergency therapy, a first-aid approach designed to stanch the bleeding.

Most couples have no idea when they stopped doing what once enriched their marriage. Feeling trapped and hurt, they forget how often they used to communicate at a heart level, how they used to make time for one another, how they formerly shared spiritual experiences, such as prayer and church attendance. They know only that their satisfaction in marriage has plunged and that the relationship now feels oppressive and bitter, or unfulfilling and second-rate.

Consider just one crucial activity—getting to know one another—that characterizes all happy couples. Human beings are incredibly complex creatures, and no one can hope to "know" another in only a few years (or decades!). If husbands and wives don't continue to enlarge their pool of knowledge concerning each other, unmet expectations are bound to cause them trouble.

PROMISED LAND TIP
Regularly think back to the fun times, happy moments, and memorable outings. Reminisce about activities that strengthened your marriage and things that you enjoy. Start doing those things again.

Countless studies prove that unrealized or unfulfilled expectations contribute to a big chunk of marriage dissatisfaction. And the problem is, when you stop talking, these expectations remain unknown or unspoken. We should be earning a Ph.D. in our spouses, but too often we drop that difficult course of study and fall back on what we think our spouse *ought* to be like.

I grew up in a home in which my mom cooked breakfast for me every morning. She always got up early, singing cheerfully and chatting with me about the day to come. Her habit might have irritated me a little, but that's what she did every morning, and I came to expect it. I never thought about it; I never even paid attention to it. I just naturally assumed that's what moms and wives did. They showed love by cooking breakfast.

It never occurred to me that Erin might have a very different expectation.

After Erin and I returned home from our honeymoon and got settled in our new apartment, I expected breakfast to appear on our table.

Erin slept in.

I remember thinking, *Wow, she slept in. I have to get breakfast on my own.* But I gave her the benefit of the doubt. *It's our first morning home,* I thought, *and she's tired.*

But the second morning, the same thing happened. I got up at eight—and found no one there to fix my breakfast. My bride slept in until about ten o'clock. I had to make it myself *again* and didn't get to enjoy the fellowship I expected with Erin.

I soon started to worry that something had gone terribly wrong. After a week went by, I sat down with Erin and said, "Are you mad at me?"

She cocked her head and asked, "What are you talking about?"

"Well," I answered, "I've noticed that you haven't gotten up with me early in the morning and cooked breakfast."

"What?"

I stammered and then continued. "Well . . . yeah. My mom used to cook breakfast for me."

Even as the words came out of my mouth, I realized that this had been an expectation that we never once discussed as a couple. My wife laughed and replied, "Greg, if you want a hot meal, I'll light your Corn Flakes on fire."

Sadly, many unmet expectations don't result in laughter. Failure to talk about issues close to our hearts may well lead to the bitterness of soul or deflation of spirit that characterizes marital slavery.

DON'T START DOING HARMFUL THINGS

We descend into misery not only when we stop doing positive things but also when we start doing negative things. Unhealthy patterns contribute to the downward slope that leads to troubled marriages.

Perhaps the biggest culprits in this parade of negativity are what I call "relationship germs." These relational microbes can invade the healthiest of marriages and leave them sick and dying. All of these germs use the same entry point: open wounds caused by everyday conflict. The excellent research of marriage experts Dr. Scott Stanley, Dr. Howard Markman, and Dr. Susan Blumberg has identified four deadly relationship germs. These four germs, similar to the patterns Dr. John Gottman has identified as marriage killers, destroy more marriages than any other relationship pathogen.[1]

Germ 1: Withdrawal

Many husbands and wives (although usually it's the husband) withdraw whenever a conflict erupts. They do not want to discuss it, they do not want to mention it; they simply leave, either physically or emotionally.

When a guy's heartbeat rises above about a hundred beats per minute (seventy is normal), he goes into fight-or-flight mode. During conflict, a man's heart rate naturally rises much faster than a woman's. His usually gets above a hundred long before his wife's does—and that's why a lot of men withdraw. They're already in the fight-or-flight mode. So usually they fly.

Habitual withdrawal as a way to cope with conflict is a high predictor of divorce. Why? If spouses withdraw from a conflict, they don't ever solve it. They might try to work out the problem separately or hit the Reset button and try to return the relationship to the status quo, but they never solve anything. And in time that often leads to divorce.

Withdrawal may not look like one of the most damaging relationship germs, but it is. Many couples infected with the germ never seem to argue. When feelings get hurt, one or both partners ignore the pain and hope the negative feelings will just go away.

They don't.

When someone withdraws from conflict, he or she only delays the inevitable. It doesn't help to leave the battlefield and go out for a long jog; in fact, this usually makes things worse. When we avoid conflict, we merely brush the hurt under the rug of our soul. Eventually the mound of hurt gets so big that it starts spilling out the sides—and what seeps out often looks a lot like anger, bitterness, depression, drug and alcohol abuse, eating disorders, or worse.

Germ 2: Escalation

When some husbands and wives face conflict, they escalate; that is, they increase the intensity and volume of their conflict. It's probably safe to say that these couples fight rather than just argue. Couples who escalate during conflict tend to yell and scream at one another. The fight spirals out of control. This is the "fight" part of the fight-or-flight mode.

This germ is all about adrenaline. Couples infected with the escalation germ tend to scream and escalate their arguments to the point where neither spouse thinks rationally. This germ tends to make arguments vicious. When the blood starts boiling, partners say things they do not mean and cannot take back.

Such arguments end up looking like a war zone—but neither side ever wins.

A friend of mine once house-sat for a couple who planned to be away for three weeks. He spent a day and a half with this pair before they left on their trip. My friend says, "It was the most uncomfortable thirty-six hours of my life." Why? This unhappy husband and wife had made escalation an art form.

It would go something like this. The husband, who did most of the cooking, would notice that one of his favorite spatulas hadn't been washed thoroughly. He'd look over at his wife and say, "This hasn't been washed."

"Yes it has," she'd say.

"I say it hasn't!"

"Then wash it to your heart's content."

"You can't clean anything right!"

"What would you know about clean? You're the one who makes all the messes!"

"I'll make a mess of *you!*"

"Yeah? Well, you're *already* a mess!"

"Why, you %#@!"

"You *#@+!! You stupid, lazy, #$@@!!"

And they'd be off and running. My friend spent as much of those thirty-six hours as possible taking long walks in the neighborhood, just to get away from the toxic atmosphere of the home.

Germ 3: Belittling

This germ leaves a sour taste in our mouths. Those infected with it call each other insulting names or use demeaning language.

"Who thinks like you? God gave you a pea-sized brain."

"Our dog has more manners than you do."

"You're one taco short of a combination plate."

Hurtful remarks stick. And who wants to hang on to a relationship in which they're constantly belittled? Plenty of times Erin and I have said things to one another and afterward asked, "Why did I say that? What a terrible thing to say!" But it can't be taken back.

When we belittle our spouses with our words, we devalue and dishonor them. We make them feel less than wonderful. We put ourselves above our spouses, looking down on them, as if they hold an inferior position to us with opinions, feelings, or needs not nearly so important as our own. Like the other germs, this one can kill.

Germ 4: Negative Beliefs

I consider this germ the most brutal of all. Negative beliefs infect us when we start to believe a lie about our spouse, when we accept as true something far more negative than it really is.

Negative beliefs cause so much destruction because of a phenomenon called *confirmation bias*. Confirmation bias finds evidence to support a person's beliefs—whether positive or negative—in everything the other person does. We look for evidence to confirm our negative biases.

If a husband believes his wife is purposely ruining their relationship, he'll notice and focus on everything she does that appears negative. At the same time, he'll neglect or reinterpret all the contrary evidence. If he sees her doing something positive, he'll say to himself, "She's doing that only so she can spend more time on herself. She is *so* selfish!" Both positive and negative events may occur throughout the day, but either he doesn't see the good or he reframes it as chance or as manipulation. He continues to focus on the negative, which becomes his evidence. He'll point friends to his jar of evidence and say, "Do you *see* what I'm living with?" And his friends likely will agree: "Ughh—you're right."

Confirmation bias happens all the time. A short while ago Erin and I were going to buy a Honda Civic. The moment we said, "Let's get a Civic," we saw the model all over town. Civics seemed to be everywhere. And I thought, *Man, there's a run on Civics in the city. We have to get one now!* The Civics, of course, already were there; I just hadn't been looking for them. The moment I started watching for Civics, I found them, and that shaped my vision.

Whatever we believe, we look for evidence to support our belief, and once we find the evidence, our discovery shapes the way we behave and react.

Do you see how destructive this germ can be? Imagine a wife who sees her husband as mean-spirited and unloving. She interprets all of his behavior through that negative filter. Therefore nothing her husband does will measure up because she's already tried and convicted him. Suppose that one day he brings home flowers, just to encourage her. When he knocks to surprise her and she opens the door, she starts sobbing. Confused, he asks the reason for her tears. "I've had a horrible day at home, the kids are still screaming, the dishwasher broke," she says, "and now you come home *drunk!*"

These four germs can infect your marriage, and if you don't take steps to treat the disease they cause, they can launch you down the road to divorce. No one has a natural immunity to them, and if you don't learn the healthy coping skills that I'll outline in coming chapters, these germs will overpower your marriage and send you into a downward spiral.

Not sure how seriously these germs may have infected your relationship? Then take the following simple test to find out.[2] Read each of the statements listed below, and write down the number that best describes how often you feel you and your spouse experience what the statements describe. Use a three-point scale: 1 = almost never; 2 = once in a while; 3 = frequently. When you finish, total your score:

SELF-TEST TO DISCOVER GERMS THAT INFECT YOUR MARRIAGE

GERM	SCORE
1. When we argue, one of us withdraws, not wanting to talk about it anymore, or leaves the scene.	_____
2. Little arguments escalate into ugly fights, with accusations, criticisms, name-calling, or bringing up past hurts.	_____

GERM	SCORE
3. My partner criticizes or belittles my opinions, feelings, or desires.	_____
4. My partner seems to view my words or actions more negatively than I mean them to be.	_____
5. When we have a problem to solve, it is as if we are on opposite teams.	_____
6. I hold back from telling my partner what I really think and feel.	_____
7. I think seriously about what it would be like to date or marry someone else.	_____
8. I feel lonely in this relationship.	_____
	TOTAL _____

What Does This Mean?

These statements, aimed at identifying the communication and conflict-management patterns that predict trouble in a relationship, are based on fifteen years of research completed at the University of Denver. Dr. Scott Stanley and Dr. Howard Markman conducted a nationwide, random phone survey using these statements. The average score was 11; higher scores mean your relationship may be in even greater danger.

GREEN LIGHT: SCORE OF 8–12

If you scored in the 8–12 range, your relationship is probably in good or even great shape *at this time*. I emphasize "at this time" because relationships never stand still. In the next twelve months, you'll have either a stronger, happier relationship or one sliding in the other direction. If you scored in this range, think of it as a green light *for now* and keep moving forward to make your relationship all it can be.

YELLOW LIGHT: SCORE OF 13–17

If you scored in the 13–17 range, think of it as a yellow caution light. While you may feel happy in your relationship, your score reveals warning signs, pointing to patterns you don't want to get worse. You ought to take action to protect and improve what you have. Spending time to strengthen your relationship now may be the best thing you can do for your future together.

RED LIGHT: SCORE OF 18–24

If you scored in the 18–24 range, think of it as a red light. Stop and look at where the two of you are headed. Your score indicates the presence of patterns that could put your relationship at significant risk. You may be heading for trouble—or perhaps you're already there. But there is good news! You can stop *now* and learn ways to improve your relationship. If your dream is turning into a nightmare, don't just pull the sheets over your head. Wake up and take action!

What should you do if you notice the strong presence of one or more of these four germs? Seek help and counsel at once. If you see pyramids of pain, camels of contention, and sandy Saharas of dissension, then take my word for it—you're in Egypt. You may be stuck in a bitter and hard place. And you need deliverance.

COMMON CHARACTERISTICS OF ENSLAVED MARRIAGES

Someone has said, "Learn from the mistakes of others; you won't live long enough to make them all yourself." Good advice. Let's see what we can learn from couples who've already landed in Egypt.

To identify the most common problem issues for couples, marriage expert Dr. David Olson and his team analyzed 21,501 married couples. The top ten issues married couples identified came from six relationship areas: conflict resolution, couple flexibility, personality issues, communication, leisure activities, and parenting. See the chart for the percentage of couples who experienced the top ten stumbling blocks in their marriages.[3]

TOP TEN STUMBLING BLOCKS FOR MARRIED COUPLES

1. We have problems sharing leadership equally 93%
2. My partner is sometimes too stubborn. 87%
3. Having children reduces our marital satisfaction 84%
4. My partner is too negative or critical. 83%
5. I wish my partner had more time and energy for recreation with me 82%
6. I wish my partner were more willing to share feelings . . 82%
7. I always end up feeling responsible for the problem . . . 81%
8. I go out of my way to avoid conflict with my partner . . 79%
9. We have difficulty completing tasks or projects 79%
10. Our differences never seem to get resolved. 78%

I did some informal research of my own to try to understand the areas of greatest struggle for newlyweds. When I asked 462 adults from Seattle, Washington, to name the most difficult part of their first year of marriage, I made some interesting discoveries. Listed below are the top five areas, with specific responses under each.

#1 ANSWER: ADJUSTING OR ADAPTING TO THE MARRIAGE
- Getting over the honeymoon phase to develop a realistic view of married life.
- Adjusting to the other person's habits.
- Getting used to someone's always being there.
- Adapting to each other's feelings and ways of doing things.
- Realizing that dating and marriage are very different.

#2 ANSWER: UNDERSTANDING THE DIFFERENCES (OR PERSONALITY DIFFERENCES)
- Blending personalities, not trying to make the other conform to my way of thinking.
- Discovering our differences and the conflict it produced; it seemed that we had so much in common before marriage.

- Having different ideas of how we plan or make decisions or even just run a household.
- Understanding and accepting/resolving our cultural differences.
- Resolving differences in belief and standards for parenting.

#3 ANSWER: DEALING WITH EXPECTATIONS
- Accepting very different expectations.
- Getting blindsided by unspoken expectations.
- Discussing and handling unrealistic expectations.
- Realizing that expectations and reality are far apart.

#4 ANSWER: DEALING WITH CONFLICT AND COMMUNICATION PROBLEMS
- Dealing with my spouse's withdrawal into moody silence for days anytime I tried to talk about problems.
- Handling the conflicts that got out of control so fast.
- Feeling cut off, cut out, constantly criticized, belittled, and worthless.
- Not knowing how to resolve our conflicts.

#5 ANSWER: DEALING WITH IN-LAWS
- Learning others' expectations and how we were not meeting them.
- Setting and maintaining boundaries.
- Breaking away from family and starting our own traditions.
- Spending appropriate time with each set of parents.
- Handling holiday expectations.

Marriages can wind up in slavery for any number of reasons, but they all have one thing in common: the discouraged partners find themselves stuck exactly where they don't want to be. It's a terrible place to live, and it doesn't get any better with time. Trust me, I know all about that awful place.

A HORSE OF A DIFFERENT PALATE

Even though Erin and I certainly enjoyed our first few years of marriage, we also found them painfully difficult. We had not yet learned how to manage conflict, and our styles clashed radically. That led to a lot of nasty arguments that we routinely failed to resolve.

Erin gets aggressive, boisterous, and emotional during conflict. I'm the opposite; conflict can easily flood my circuits and overwhelm me. Our inborn personalities give us very little common ground on which to resolve our disagreements.

Back in my school days, we didn't have a LUV talk method (see chapter 10), and we didn't do any premarital training. Even though I intended to "go into the business" of relationships, we entered marriage unprepared for the conflicts bound to come. As a result, whenever things started to go wrong, we dug a hole deeper and just kept on digging.

Eventually we reached the point where I thought we stood at the edge of a cliff, just one more conflict away from separation. I didn't believe that she would ever divorce me, but I felt certain that she had grown so thoroughly sick of me that she would leave.

During one of our difficult times, I recognized that we were not connecting and that our relationship felt awash in negativity.

"Hey," I suggested, "why don't I take the day off from school, you can take the day off from work, and we'll go on a picnic? Let's drive up into the Denver foothills, find a river, sit down, eat, and just enjoy each other."

"Great," she replied. "That's a wonderful idea."

So we put together some food, dumped everything in the truck, and started driving. Foolishly I brought up an issue that already had prompted more than one argument. I ended up saying something sarcastic and hurt her feelings. Erin turned toward the window and refused to speak to me or even look at me.

So here we were, on our way to a picnic, and she wouldn't talk. I tried to reengage Erin, to get her to speak with me, but I got nowhere fast. We were driving on an old dirt road near the picnic area, and as I rounded a sharp corner around a big boulder, I slammed on my brakes. A huge horse stood in the middle of the road.

Erin barely blinked.

"We almost hit a horse!" I yelled, pointing wildly to the animal. "There's a big horse! Hey, that's not an everyday occurrence."

I drove around next to the beast, rolled down my window, and the horse stuffed his massive head in the cab, literally knocking me back. I thought it was kind of cool and started petting the animal.

"Hey, Erin," I said. "You have to see this. We have a *horse* in the truck! That's not me breathing." She shrugged her shoulders in a "whatever" sort of way.

What is your problem? I groused.

On this outing we had been munching Funyuns and drinking diet Coke as we drove. When the horse stuck his massive head in the truck, he must have smelled the onion-flavored rings and decided to satisfy his hunger. He panned around to find the source, eventually choosing the lone treat lying in my lap. He lowered his head and bit.

I screamed bloody murder. My high-pitched squeal reached the stratosphere. The startled horse banged his head on the roof, then galloped off down the road.

In excruciating pain, I turned to Erin for support. I desperately wanted some comfort. At that point, I didn't know for sure what the horse had bit. But the moment I turned to her and saw her face, I instantly knew—*she* had put the Funyun in my lap.

"How could you?" I stammered. "I'm not going to be able to have kids now! Do you have any *idea* what just happened?"

She denied everything. "I did *not* do that," she insisted.

(To this day, we have an ongoing dispute. I tell her, "It's okay. Get it off your chest. Let it go. It will feel so much better just to finally admit that you put the Funyun in my lap." But she still denies it. I tease her that on her deathbed, she's going to pull me close and with her last breath whisper, "I put the Funyun in your lap." And I'll be vindicated.)

In the end, I wound up with a fiendishly big, black bruise on my upper thigh. That horse almost ruined me! And my argument with my wife didn't do me any good either. As you might imagine, Erin and I sank deeper into misery that day.

I'm glad to say, however, that eventually we learned the healthy coping skills that I'm about to share with you. And they must work. Despite the horse, Erin and I became the happy parents of three great kids.

(And to this day, I don't allow Funyuns anywhere near my lap.)

CHAPTER 4

DOING A DESTRUCTIVE DANCE

—•—

The people of Israel had lived in Egypt for 430 years.
EXODUS 12:40

—•—

ERIN IS A nurse, and on occasion her nursing duties require her to work the evening shift. On one such night, I felt alone and bored—and when I get bored, I like to change things.

I decided to rearrange the master bedroom. I moved the bed, repositioned the knick-knacks and their shelves, relocated the dresser, and generally gave the room a new look. Then I went to bed and turned out the lights.

Erin didn't want to wake me when she got home, so she kept the lights off. She tiptoed into the bedroom and immediately smashed her shin on a little table that, until a few hours before, hadn't been there. She tripped and crashed into a pair of antique skis, which in turn tumbled onto a shelf containing all her beloved Precious Moments figurines. The skis shattered most of her treasures, then continued to fall until they smacked into my head.

The combination of breaking glass, falling objects, my wife screaming, and a blow to the skull made me think, *Robbery!* Now it was fight or flight—and in the dark, I had no desire to fight anyone. Instead I bolted from bed, forgot that I had moved everything, and ran straight into the wall, bloodying my nose.

When the lights came on, Erin instantly criticized me for moving the furniture without first talking about it. Her angry words made me feel like a failure, so I started to defend myself. I minimized her concerns, rejected her opinions, and made the argument ten times worse.

Does any of this sound the least bit familiar?

As Erin and I look back, we see a similar vicious cycle playing out in every major argument of our marriage. We recognized the pattern early on, but we didn't know how to break it. Either she or I withdrew, and while things eventually calmed down, we always seemed to return to the same frustrating spot. To try to move ahead, we learned some good communication skills and became adept at putting pieces back together, but still we could not get over the hump. We simply could not understand why our discussions so often ended in explosions. We seemed to act out the very same script, time after time.

"When I say that we need to talk about something like this," Erin would say, "or I bring up something that shows where you haven't done such a good job, why does it bother you so much?"

"I have no idea," I would reply. "It just does. And why, when I start to explain myself, does that bother *you* so much?"

"I don't know, but it just does."

Our habits didn't change for the better until we finally understood that we had become mired in a destructive relationship dance. Not until we recognized that certain identifiable "buttons" tend to set us off, starting us on yet another futile round of accusations, attacks, and rationalizations, did we begin to find our way out of the drudgery of Egypt. We remained shackled until at last we got a handle on our unique relationship dance.

A LONG TIME IN CHAINS

You know one of the worst things about slavery? You can't get out of it just any old time you please. A slave can't simply say, "Well, I'm tired of all this forced labor nonsense. I've had enough of whips and overseers. See you later; I'm out of here."

Slaves get stuck in slavery, usually for an excruciatingly long time. The Bible tells us that the Israelites languished in Egypt for 430 years. For the better part of four tedious centuries, God's chosen people served under the lash of their brutal Egyptian overlords.

And what finally led to their freedom? Their pain! Listen to the Scripture: "Years passed, and the king of Egypt died. But the Israelites still groaned beneath their burden of slavery. They cried out for help, and their pleas for deliverance rose up to God. God heard their cries and remembered his covenant promise to Abraham, Isaac, and Jacob. He looked down on the Israelites and felt deep concern for their welfare" (Exodus 2:23-25).

The Israelites stayed stuck in Egyptian slavery for centuries until the pain grew so intense that they cried out to God for relief. While none of us lives for 430 years, the pain we endure while remaining stuck in marital drudgery can feel centuries long. Many who refuse to go the route of divorce or separation nevertheless spend a lifetime in bondage. They're stuck.

Statistics tell us that about 50 percent of those who marry today will wind up in divorce court. And of the 50 percent who stay together, only about 25 percent of those will feel satisfied with their relationship.[1] So when you combine the half who leave and the quarter who feel dissatisfied, only about 12 percent of married couples ever find anything close to what they want. The rest remain stuck.

I contend that there's a very particular reason *why* they're stuck. They get trapped by their own relationship dance and cannot break free of it. The marriage intensives conducted at the Smalley Marriage Institute work, to a large degree, because we help couples to identify and break the rhythm of their own dance. And when that happens, these couples discover an exodus of their own.

Couples who come to the Smalley Marriage Institute for a marriage intensive almost always get a big surprise early in our sessions. Their mouths fly open, and we can usually hear them take in a quick breath when, after just a couple of hours, we sketch out on a whiteboard their own unique dance.

"That's *it!*" they exclaim, amazed. "That's exactly what we do! If we didn't know better, we would think you guys are living with us! "

In truth, we don't have any crystal balls. We haven't even placed hidden microphones or cameras around the couples' houses. But we have done some assessment before meeting the couples in person, so usually we can very quickly nail their unique relational dance. I've done the same thing with couples planning to get married, and many of them look at me, big lumps in their throats, and ask somberly, "Then should we be getting married?" I tell all of them that the buttons are not the problem. Most of our buttons, I believe, have been with us from childhood.[2]

The buttons are not the problem. The problem is how we choose to cope with them. So I explain to worried couples, "Some of the ways you're coping with your buttons right now are problematic. I'd say they're red flags. I'd also say that if you keep doing things this way over the course of years, you're going to put your relationship at risk."

The truth is, the buttons that set us off existed even when the marriage was going well, even during our engagement, even when we began dating. But when our buttons got pushed in those early days, we didn't normally respond in problematic ways. And even if we did cope in an unhealthy fashion, our partner's rose-colored glasses made our unpleasant response seem not quite so negative or overwhelming. Once the marriage gets stuck, however, we often become slaves to our unique dance.

THE ORIGINAL BUTTON

My colleague Bob Paul has helped me to understand that at the core of this dance lies a button of fear. That fear may take many shapes: fear of failure, fear of abandonment, fear of rejection, fear of inadequacy, fear of you-name-it.

And from where does this fear come? If you reread the Creation story in Genesis with a fresh pair of eyes, I believe you can see some telling evidence that points to the source of this "fear button."

After God created Adam and Eve, he informed them about two special trees blossoming in the middle of the Garden: the tree of life and the tree of the knowledge of good and evil. Regarding the first, God gave no commandment. But of the second he said, "You must not eat from the tree of the knowledge of good and evil, for when you eat of it you will surely die" (Genesis 2:17, NIV).

This story has long fascinated me. Why did God create a perfect Garden—Eden, a place where sin had never entered—and put there an object capable of paving the way for staggering pain? Why did God plant this thing in Eden and then tell his creatures not to eat its fruit? Why not just leave the tree out of the Garden altogether?

I think God did this because he created the man and woman to depend on him, not to live an autonomous life apart from him. God apparently gave the command to not eat of the tree so that we wouldn't become self-sufficient and insist on stubborn control of our own lives.

The moment that Adam heard God's warning (and the moment Eve heard it repeated), I imagine he felt some fear. "*Die? Death?* You mean, like being separated from God—from life? Are you saying that Eve could *die,* the very one with whom I have come to lovingly connect on a deep physical and emotional level? You mean she could be taken from me? I can't think of anything more dreadful. I would be left alone forever!"

I can't prove it, of course, but I believe such a scenario accurately reflects the psychological condition of Adam and Eve before the Fall. It makes even more sense to me when I see that it was precisely this fear that Satan exploited with Eve. The serpent encouraged her to eat the forbidden fruit with the false reassurance, "You won't die!" (Genesis 3:4).

When Satan recognized Eve's fear of death and disconnection, he cunningly said to her, in effect, "Oh please, don't worry about that. You're not going to get cut off. As a matter of fact, God just doesn't want you to become like him, knowing everything and being in control."

Eve chose to cope with her deepest fear of separation from God, self, and others by taking control of her life. The instant she ate of the forbidden fruit, she became autonomous and tried to become self-sufficient. She no longer had to depend on God for wisdom.

Of course, her strategy of coping with fear didn't work. In fact, her fear of separation and disconnection became a self-fulfilling prophecy: because of her choice to try to become self-sufficient (sin), God cast her out of the Garden. Thus Eve forfeited eternal connection with God for the opportunity to control her own life. Adam made the same choice and suffered the same consequence: immediate separation from God.

The two fears highlighted by this ancient story remain, even today, the two deepest, core fears plaguing modern men and women: We fear being disconnected, and we fear not being in control. We still think that acquiring knowledge gives us control—and if knowledge is power, then we want omniscience. We seek knowledge as a way to avoid being helpless. If I'm like God, then I control my own life and no longer have to depend on him. I'm no longer helpless and don't have to worry about disconnection from relationships.

But it doesn't quite work out that way, does it? Satan lied. Adam and Eve *did* die, and they *were* disconnected from their choicest relationships. And yet, somehow, even though we know what happened to them, we still fall prey to the two core fears that Satan exploited to destroy our first parents. And most often, those two fears find expression in what I like to call the Fear Dance.

HOW THE FEAR DANCE WORKS

Most people have one primary fear. Of the hundreds of couples I've counseled and the thousands I've surveyed, almost all have one core fear. When someone pushes that fear button and the other person responds with unhealthy reactions, the two people begin a destructive dance.

My greatest fear is the fear of failure. If I feel I'm failing—or even if I feel I'm at risk for failure—I cope with that feeling by turning to certain unhealthy strategies..

Even as a kid, I remember fearing failure. I have a mild reading disability. In the sixth grade my teacher asked me to read out loud. I tried, and I sounded like an idiot. All the kids laughed at me and called me Retard and Dork. I remember feeling like a total failure. To this day, I break out into a cold sweat if someone asks me to read out loud.

If my wife is the one who pushes my Fear-of-Failure button, I respond by pushing her button. She then reacts by pushing my button again, but perhaps even harder this time. And so we begin a hurtful dance, an endless cycle that goes 'round and 'round.

Suppose Erin says, "Greg, we need to sit down and talk about last night." Immediately I feel the pressure of her finger on my fear button. I already feel as if I've done something wrong. "When you came home an hour late from work and didn't have the courtesy to call me," she continues, "that really bothered me."

In that moment I feel as if I have failed as a husband. And so I instantly try to cope with that fear. I attempt to take control, perhaps by defending myself.

"Give me a break," I say. "An *hour?* I got stuck in traffic. I mean, come *on.* What's the big deal?"

Or maybe I'll attack: "You know, you're late, too. You're late all the time. But I don't bring that up, do I?"

Or perhaps I'll minimize her concern: "With all the real problems we face, why are we even talking about *this?*"

I try to cope with my feeling of failure by trying to make myself feel successful. More accurately, I try to get *Erin* to make me feel successful.

But when I use unhealthy reactions I only end up pushing my wife's button. In Erin's case, her button is a fear that I will not value her feelings, opinions, beliefs, and thoughts. She needs to be valued and validated. When she says, "Greg, it really hurt my feelings when you didn't call me last night," she's hoping that I'll validate her by saying, "You're right. I'm so sorry. By not calling you, I can see how that offends you and feels hurtful. Maybe you felt worried, maybe you had a special dinner waiting for me—and how inconsiderate that was for me not even to call."

When Erin starts to feel invalidated—when I push her fear button—she may go into attack mode. But she isn't attacking me for the sake of attacking. Instead, she is hoping her actions will prompt me to validate her. But when she attacks, I feel like an even worse failure. And so the dance continues, in an ever-widening circle.

This Fear Dance keeps couples stuck in slavery. Every husband and wife team, to whatever degree, has some kind of dance. (Actually, people in *any* kind of close relationship tend to develop their own Fear Dance. The book I coauthored with the Relationship Revolution team, *The DNA of Relationships*, shows how the Fear Dance applies to many other kinds of relationships.) Sometimes the Fear Dance hasn't reached destructive levels—most commonly, with young marrieds or the engaged—but if the Fear Dance is not addressed, it can send even the happiest couple into misery.

The very fact that couples engage in the Fear Dance shows us that both partners want something. I, for example, want to feel successful and to avoid failure. Erin wants to feel valued for who she is, for her feelings, and for what she thinks. When we cue up the grating music and start our Fear Dance, we labor under the illusion that by coping in such unhealthy ways, we'll get what we really want. But it never works out that way. Let me give you an example.

Erin and I normally sit down and decide together how often I travel on business. Recently she said to me, "Greg, we have to talk about this. This is not going well. You're traveling way too much. Our kids are suffering, I'm suffering." She didn't intend to attack; she simply wanted to begin a much-needed conversation.

But what happened inside of me? Here's how I interpreted her words: "You are failing me as a husband. You're failing our children as a father. You're one big failure." The moment she spoke, I began to defend myself.

"First of all," I retorted, "before you even *start* in on this, let me remind you that we made all these decisions *together*. My travel schedule is as much your decision as it is mine. So whatever you're trying to say, don't make it sound as if it's my fault."

Erin had been hoping that I would validate her by saying something like, "Honey, you have a great ability to sense our family. You can tell when things aren't going well. So even though we decided on this schedule together, I see that we need to reevaluate."

But did I validate her? Unfortunately not. I worried more about trying to feel successful than I did about her need for validation. And so our dance began in earnest.

As soon as I pushed her button, she responded by pushing mine. "Hey, why can't you ever just listen? Why do you have to argue and defend yourself every time we have a discussion?"

Again, I felt like a failure. So now I rationalized: "You know what? This is what I do for a job. How do you think money gets into our bank account? How does food get put on the table? If I'm not traveling, how do these things happen? What do you want me to do?"

The ultimate problem with such a diseased cycle is that it breeds total dependency. The Fear Dance causes me to believe (wrongly) that my wife is both the problem and the solution. *If she just didn't attack me,* I think, *I wouldn't need to defend myself. If she would just calmly sit down, if only she would remind me of all the things that I do right, I wouldn't get so upset.* When I see Erin as both the problem and the solution, I become totally dependent on her. And the same thing happens to her with me.

I remain totally dependent on Erin when I think that if only she would understand me and act in a way consistent with that understanding, then everything would be fine. She remains totally dependent on me when she thinks that if only I would understand her and act in a way consistent with that understanding, then all would be well. As long as we both believe that the other holds the key to our success, we each remain totally dependent on the other.

IDENTIFYING FEAR BUTTONS

Are you ready to try to discover and name your fear buttons? What follows should help you to identify the Fear Dance unique to you and your spouse. I've successfully used this survey in various settings to help couples get to the essence of their dance. By the time you've worked through it, you should be able to describe and draw your own dance, just as I do with couples at a marriage intensive.

Pay special attention to the survey's key question: "How did you feel about yourself in the middle of this conflict?" The question is not merely, "How did you feel?" ("I felt hurt, frustrated, angry.") Rather, the central question is, "When you felt hurt or frustrated, how did that make you feel *about yourself?*"

> ────────○────── ──
> **PROMISED LAND TIP**
> Clearly identify the
> buttons that are driving
> your Fear Dance.
> ── ──────○───────

Because it's important for both spouses to discover their buttons, we have placed a copy of this survey in appendix A at the back of the book. You can take the survey in one of two ways: (1) you can write in the book (one spouse writing here and one writing in appendix A); or (2) you can make two photocopies of the survey in appendix A and both write on the photocopies.

IDENTIFYING YOUR FEAR DANCE

1. Describe a recent conflict or negative situation with your spouse—something that really "pushed your button." For the purpose of this exercise, be sure that you and your spouse write down the *same conflict.*

_____

_____

_____

2. How did this conflict make you feel about *yourself?* What did the conflict say about *you?* What was the *"self"* message—the message that it sent to *you?* What were the *buttons* that got pushed? Look through the options and use them to fill in the blanks in this statement: As a result of the above conflict, I felt _____ or feared feeling _____ Check all that apply—but "star" the most important feeling:

✓ or *	"As a result of the conflict, I felt . . ."	What That Feeling Sounds Like
	Rejected	I will be discarded; I will be seen as useless; my spouse doesn't need me; I am not necessary in this relationship; my spouse doesn't desire intimacy with me.
	Unwanted	My spouse doesn't want me; my mate will not choose me; my spouse is staying in the marriage out of duty, obligation, or because it's the "right" thing to do.
	Abandoned	I will be alone; my spouse will ultimately leave me; my spouse won't be committed to me for life.
	Disconnected	We will become emotionally detached or separated; there are walls or barriers between us in the marriage.
	Like a failure	I am not successful at being a husband/wife; I will not perform right or correctly; I will fall short in my relationship; I won't make the grade.
	Helpless or powerless	I cannot do anything to change my spouse or my situation; I do not possess the power, resources, capacity, or ability to get what I want.

✓ or *	"As a result of the conflict, I felt . . ."	What That Feeling Sounds Like
	Controlled	I will be controlled by my spouse; my mate will exercise authority over me; I will be made to "submit;" my spouse will restrain me; I will be treated like a child or my mate will act like my parent.
	Defective	Something is wrong with me; I'm the problem; I am unlovable.
	Inadequate	I am not capable; I am incompetent.
	Inferior	Everyone else is better than I am; I am less valuable or important than others.
	Invalidated	Who I am, what I think, what I do, or how I feel is not valued by my spouse.
	Unloved	My spouse doesn't love me anymore; my spouse has no affection or desire for me; my relationship lacks warm attachment, admiration, enthusiasm, or devotion.
	Dissatisfied	I will not experience satisfaction within the relationship; I will exist in misery for the rest of my life; I will not be pleased within my marriage; I feel no joy in my relationship.
	Taken advantage of	I will be cheated by my spouse; my partner will take advantage of me; my spouse will withhold something I need; I will feel like a doormat; I won't get what I want.
	Worthless or devalued	I am useless; my spouse fails to recognize my value and worth; I feel cheapened or undervalued in the relationship; I have little or no value to my spouse; my mate does not see me as priceless.
	Cheated	My spouse will take advantage of me; my spouse will withhold something I need; I won't get what I want.

✓ or *	"As a result of the conflict, I felt . . ."	What That Feeling Sounds Like
	Not good enough	Nothing I do is ever acceptable, satisfactory, or sufficient for my spouse; I always have more "hoops" to jump through; I will never be able to meet my spouse's expectations of me; my efforts will never be enough.
	Unaccepted	My spouse does not accept me; my partner is not pleased with me; my spouse does not approve of me.
	Judged	I am always being unfairly judged or misjudged; my spouse forms faulty or negative opinions about me; I am always being evaluated; my spouse does not approve of me.
	Humiliated	This marriage is extremely destructive to my self-respect or dignity.
	Ignored	My spouse will not pay attention to me; I feel neglected.
	Unimportant	I am not important to my spouse; I am irrelevant, insignificant, or of little priority to my spouse.
	Useless	I am of no use in my marriage; I am ineffective; I am not needed.
	Afraid of intimacy	I am afraid of opening up emotionally to my spouse; I will be hurt emotionally if I allow my spouse past my walls.
	Misunderstood	My spouse will fail to understand me correctly; my spouse will get the wrong idea or impression about me; I will be misinterpreted or misread.
	Misportrayed	My spouse has an inaccurate protrayal of me; I am misrepresented or represented in a false way; I am described in a negative or untrue manner; my spouse paints a wrong picture of me; my spouse has negative beliefs about me.

✓ or *	"As a result of the conflict, I felt . . ."	What That Feeling Sounds Like
	Disrespected	I will be insulted; my spouse does not admire me; my spouse will have a low opinion of me; I will be disregarded; my spouse does not respect me; my spouse does not look up to me.
	Out of control	My marriage will be wild, unruly, or hectic; my spouse will be unmanageable or uncontrollable; things will feel disorganized or in disorder.
	Alone	I will be by myself or on my own; I will be without help or assistance; I will be lonely; I will be isolated.
	Insignificant	I am irrelevant in the relationship; I am not necessary in my marriage; my spouse does not see me as an important part of our relationship.
	Unknown	My spouse will not know me; I will feel like a stranger to my spouse; I will be nameless or anonymous to my partner; I will be unfamilar to my spouse.
	As if I'm boring	There will be no passion in our marriage; my spouse perceives me as dull and dreary; our marriage is uninteresting; my spouse will believe that he or she knows everything there is to know about me; I feel as if we are just roommates; there will be no romantic feelings between us.
	Like a disappointment	I will be a letdown in the marriage; my spouse will be disppointed in me; my spouse will be disillusioned by me.
	Phony	My spouse will see me as fake or not genuine; my mate will believe that I'm a fraud, pretender, or an imposter; my spouse will perceive that I'm not who I say I am.

✓ or *	"As a result of the conflict, I felt . . ."	What That Feeling Sounds Like
	Other:	

3. What do you *do* when you feel _____
[insert the most important feeling from question #2]? How do
you *react* when you feel that way? Identify your common *coping
strategies* to deal with that feeling. Check all that apply—but
"star" the most important coping behaviors:

✓ or *	"When I am in Conflict I . . ."	Explanation
	Withdraw	You avoid others or alienate yourself without resolution; you are distant; you sulk or use the silent treatment.
	Stonewall	You turn into a stone wall by not responding to your spouse.
	Escalate	Your emotions spiral out of control; you argue, raise your voice, fly into a rage.
	Emotionally shut down	You detach emotionally and close your heart towards your spouse; you "numb out"; you become devoid of emotion; you have no regard for others' needs or troubles.
	Pacify	You try to soothe, calm down, or placate your spouse; you try to get your spouse to not feel negative emotions.
	Try to earn love	You try to do more to earn others' love and care.
	Belittle	You devalue or dishonor someone with words or actions; you call your spouse names, use insults, ridicule, take potshots at or mock him or her.

✓ or *	"When I am in Conflict I . . ."	Explanation
	Indulge in negative beliefs	You believe your spouse is far worse than is really the case; you see your spouse in a negative light or attribute negative motives to him or her; you see your spouse through a negative lens.
	Become arrogant	You posture yourself as superior, better than, or wiser than your spouse.
	Blame	You place responsibility on others, not accepting fault; you're convinced the problem is your spouse's fault.
	Become the innocent victim	You see your spouse as an attacking monster and yourself as put upon, unfairly accused, mistreated, or unappreciated.
	Control	You hold back, restrain, oppress, or dominate your spouse; you "rule over" your spouse; you talk over or prevent your spouse from having a chance to explain his or her position, opinions, or feelings.
	Use dishonesty	You lie, withhold information, or give out false impressions; you falsify your thoughts, feelings, habits, likes, dislikes, personal history, daily activities, or plans for the future.
	Withhold	You withhold your affections, feelings, sexual intimacy, or love from your spouse.
	Demand	You try to force your mate to do something, usually with implied threat of punishment if they refuse.
	Become annoying	You use irritating habits or activities to infuriate, annoy, upset, or to get on your spouse's nerves.
	Provoke	You intentionally aggravate, hassle, goad, or irritate your spouse.
	Isolate	You shut down and go into seclusion or into your "cave."

✓ or *	"When I am in Conflict I . . ."	Explanation
	Exaggerate	You make overstatements or enlarge your words beyond bounds or the truth; you make statements like "You always . . ." or "You never . . ."
	Throw tantrums	You have a fit of bad temper; you become irritable, crabby, or grumpy.
	Deny	You refuse to admit the truth or reality.
	Invalidate	You devalue your spouse; you do not appreciate who your partner is, what he or she feels or thinks or does.
	Maintain distressing thoughts	You replay the argument over and over; you don't stop thinking about the conflict or your spouse's frustrating or hurtful behavior.
	Independent	You become separate from your spouse in your attitude, behavior, and decision making.
	Rewrite history	You recast your earlier times together in a negative light; your recall of previous disappointments and slights becomes dramatically enhanced.
	Become defensive	Instead of listening, you defend yourself by providing an explanation; you make excuses for your actions.
	Become clingy	You develop a strong emotional attachment or dependence on your spouse; you hold tight to your spouse.
	Become passive-aggressive	You display negative emotions, resentment, and aggression in passive ways, such as procrastination, forgetfulness, and stubbornness.
	Avoid	You get involved in activities to avoid your spouse.

✓ or *	"When I am in Conflict I . . ."	Explanation
	Take care of others	You become responsible for others by giving physical or emotional care and support to the point you are doing everything for your spouse, and your partner does nothing to care for himself or herself.
	Become pessimistic	You become negative, distrustful, cynical, and skeptical in your view of your spouse and marriage.
	Act out	You engage in negative behaviors like drug or alcohol abuse, extramarital affairs, excessive shopping, or overeating.
	Go into fix-it mode	You focus almost exclusively on what is needed to solve the problem.
	Complain	You express unhappiness or make accusations.
	Criticize	You pass judgment, condemn, or point out your spouse's faults; you attack his or her personality or character.
	Strike out	You lash out in anger, become verbally or physically aggressive, possibly abusive.
	Manipulate	You control, influence, or maneuver your spouse for your own advantage.
	Get angry and enraged	You display strong feelings of displeasure or violent and uncontrolled emotions.
	Catastrophize	You use dramatic, exaggerated expressions to depict that the relationship is in danger or that it has failed.
	Pursue the truth	You try to determine what really happened or who is telling the truth.
	Judge	You negatively critique, evaluate, form an opinion, or conclude something about your spouse.
	Become selfish	You become more concerned with you and your interests, feelings, wants, or desires.

✓ or *	"When I am in Conflict I . . ."	Explanation
	Lecture	You sermonize, talk down to, scold, or reprimand your spouse.
	Cross-complain	You meet your spouse's complaint (or criticism) with an immediate complaint of your own, totally ignoring what your spouse has said.
	Whine	You express yourself by using a childish, high-pitched nasal tone and stress one syllable toward the end of the sentence.
	Use negative body language	You give a false smile, shift from side to side, or fold your arms across your chest.
	Use humor	You use humor as a way of not dealing with the issue at hand.
	Become sarcastic	You use negative or hostile humor, hurtful words, belittling comments, cutting remarks, or demeaning statements.
	Minimize	You assert that your spouse is overreacting to an issue; you intentionally underestimate, downplay, or soft-pedal the issue or how your spouse feels.
	Rationalize	You attempt to make your actions seem reasonable; you try to attribute your behavior to credible motives; you try to provide believable but untrue reasons for your conduct.
	Become indifferent	You are cold and show no concern.
	Abdicate	You give away responsibilities.
	Self-depreciate	You run yourself down.
	Agree, then disagree	You start out agreeing but end up disagreeing.
	Dump	You emotionally "vomit," unload, or dump on your spouse.

✓ or *	"When I am in Conflict I . . ."	Explanation
	Become a mind reader	You make assumptions about your spouse's private feelings, behaviors, or motives.
	Repeat	You become a broken record, repeating your own position incessantly instead of understanding your spouse's position.
	Argue	You argue about who is right and who is wrong; you debate whose position is the correct or right one.
	Abandon myself	You desert or neglect yourself; you take care of everyone except yourself.
	Become indignant	You believe that you deserve to be angry, resentful, or annoyed with your spouse because of what he or she did.
	Become stubborn	You will not budge from your position; you become inflexible or persistent.
	Act righteous	You make it a moral issue or argue about issues of morality or righteousness.
	Play dumb	You pretend not to understand or know what your spouse is talking about.
	Nag	You badger, pester, or harass your spouse to do something you want.
	Other:	

UNDERSTANDING YOUR FEAR DANCE

To help you get a better idea of your own fear button, let me take you through a personal example.

1. *Describe a recent conflict or negative situation with your spouse—something that really "pushed your button."* Remember the time I decided to rearrange the master bedroom and almost killed my wife and nearly broke my nose? Well, immediately afterward, for a solid hour, Erin and I "discussed" my need to move the furniture in our bedroom.

2. *How did I feel in response to this conflict?* Erin said to me, "Why did you move our bedroom around without asking me first?" She simply wanted me to validate her frustration that I didn't first consult her. But I instantly felt *embarrassed* that she'd gotten injured and *hurt* that she was making a big deal out of an accident.

3. *How did this conflict make me feel about myself? What did the conflict say about me? What was the "self" message—the message it sent to me?* The moment that Erin started to explain her frustration, all I could hear was that I'd done something wrong, that I wasn't perfect, that I'd let her down. Her attack made me feel as if I'd failed as her husband.

4. *What do I do when I feel like a failure?* The moment I started to feel as if I'd failed as a husband, I started to *defend* myself: "Erin, I didn't know that you wanted me to seek your permission before I move furniture." I then *blamed* her: "If you want me to check things out with you before, you need to let me know these things. I'm not a mind reader." I tried to *fix the problem without listening to her feelings*: "I'll get some glue and fix your Precious Moments figurines." I might even have *minimized* her feelings: "There's no need to talk about what happened. Why are you making such a big deal out of this?" And I *rationalized:* "What happened, happened. It was just an accident."

I tried to do things that helped me feel successful. That's all I really wanted. I didn't want to feel like a failure; I wanted to feel successful as her husband.

The problem is, I used the wrong strategy to deal with my fear. I tried to control or manipulate Erin so that I could feel successful.

The moment I started to defend, blame, try to fix the problem, minimize, or rationalize, I pushed Erin's fear button. She felt invalidated. She wanted me to validate her feelings, her concerns, her frustrations. She wanted me to value the fact that she felt left out of a decision that ultimately caused her physical pain and broke her collection of figurines. So when I didn't validate her, she *escalated:* "I can't believe that you are defending yourself. You did this! I'm the one who got injured! Why won't you stop thinking about yourself and listen to me?" She *criticized* me: "You don't ever check with me before you go off and make decisions. You don't care a bit about my feelings." Then she *catastrophized* that our marriage was in dire straits. "If you can't understand that you hurt me when you disregard my opinions, then I don't have much hope for our marriage." Finally she used *sarcasm* in an attempt to get me to validate her. "Greg! I can't believe you did this. Can't you do anything right?"

And then we were off and dancing! (See the graphic for a picture of our Fear Dance.)

Each couple has a unique relational system with barriers that hinder them from having the relationship they both desire. This system, or dance, is the key to understanding what has kept you stuck in relational Egypt. Your relational dance involves a deep fear ("button") and the habitual way each of you reacts to your fear.

WHAT WERE MOSES' FEAR BUTTONS?

This survey should work for anyone who honestly wants to understand what button (or buttons) sends him or her waltzing into the Fear Dance. I believe it would work even for someone like Moses.

Moses can't take the survey, of course, but we could try to deduce his probable answers from studying the scriptural record of his life. What were his fear buttons?

The Bible appears to suggest that at various times Moses felt helpless, inadequate, worried, and frightened. And how did he feel about himself? It seems likely that he most feared inadequacy or failure. And how did he cope?

Remember when this celebrated hero encountered a burning bush? Out of that bush God's voice called Moses to lead the Israelites out of Egypt to the Promised Land. How did Moses react?

First he rationalizes: "But Moses protested again, 'Look, they won't believe me! They won't do what I tell them. They'll just say, "The Lord never appeared to you"'" (Exodus 4:1). Then Moses devalues himself: "But Moses pleaded with the Lord, 'O Lord, I'm just not a good speaker. I never have been, and I'm not now, even after you have spoken to me. I'm clumsy with words'" (Exodus 4:10). A short time later Moses abdicates: "Lord, please! Send someone else" (Exodus 4:13). Someone who deals with failure or inadequacy often abdicates by trying to give away responsibility. As I read Moses' life story, his coping mechanisms appear to remain fairly consistent.

That's not terribly surprising because the same thing is true of all of us. Our fear buttons don't normally change a great deal, no matter how long we live. We also don't change the unhealthy coping strategies that we naturally use to deal with the pushing of our buttons. That's true in my life, and it's probably true for you as well.

So what difference does any of this make? Plenty! Once you know your fear and have identified the way you normally deal with a spouse who pushes your fear button, you can take steps to stop the dance before it gets into full swing. This is a huge step toward walking out of slavery toward freedom—and as a bonus, it just might save you some embarrassment.

OF WATERFALLS AND SHOULDERS

Erin and I spent our honeymoon in Maui. I had scoured dozens of books about Hawaii, and it seemed as if every one boasted a photo of a gorgeous waterfall. These stunning pictures filled me with desire to find such a dreamlike Shangri-la, hike into it, swim there, and spend the day with my bride. It quickly became a personal mission, a compulsion, a quest.

Erin and I set out one day on an old serpentine road in the middle of nowhere. The drive made her sick, and we had to pull over so she could throw up—not exactly the picture I had in mind. Eventually we hiked about a mile away from the road and found a perfect waterfall, everything I had envisioned. As I gleefully ran into the natural pool, Erin stopped at the water's edge and refused to move.

"Let's go!" I called out.

"I can't," she replied.

I felt dumbfounded. *What* was the woman waiting for? "What are you talking about?" I asked.

She motioned for me to join her and pointed to an old, weather-beaten sign that announced No Swimming. The sign must have been eighty years old and clearly belonged to another era.

This is not possible, I thought. *Here we've found this incredible waterfall, and she's letting an old sign get in the way?*

"Honey," I said, "we're in the middle of nowhere. For one thing, who would know? For a second thing, who would care? Are they going to throw us in jail for swimming?"

By nature, Erin is not a rule breaker. And nothing I could say would convince this vision of loveliness to join me for a swim. Here we had a perfect setting, all to ourselves—you could not find a better place—and she would have none of it.

Remember, I had made it my personal quest to swim in a perfect Hawaiian water paradise. So at that moment, I felt like a failure—and I hated it. So naturally we started to argue. The argument escalated, and then I said something very foolish. "If this is the way you are going to act," I announced, "then our honeymoon is ruined."

She quit talking to me, drew on her days of running track, and fled like the wind back to our car. I couldn't keep up with her. As I trailed her, I remember thinking, *How do I tell the manager of the condo to bring a rollaway bed up to the honeymoon suite?*

The drive back to our room didn't go well. I felt like a failure, and she felt completely invalidated. We had already purchased tickets for a Polynesian dinner theater that night, but Erin remained silent while I sulked.

Somehow we communicated enough through the silence to get into the car and head to the event. When we arrived, our hosts sat us and all their guests at some long tables, as tightly as possible. We watched the performance and ate our dinners crammed shoulder to shoulder with total strangers.

And still Erin did not speak to me.

My mind began whirling with an unpleasant thought: *Man, it's getting late. I'm not going to get any intimacy tonight unless I mend this rift.* I hate to admit that I felt no compulsion to tend to her and see how I might have hurt her. I just wanted to resolve our tiff so that we could have sex.

I remembered how my dad told his seminar audiences that any time you close someone's spirit, softness can help to reopen it. *All right,* I thought, *I can do that.* I put my arm around my spouse, and I gently started to rub the top of her shoulder with the tips of my fingers.

Nothing. She didn't even acknowledge me.

What is going on here? I wondered. *This is supposed to work. Why did it work for my dad but not for me?* Despite my lack of success, I decided to keep going, this time "upping" my efforts.

Still she didn't respond with so much as a twitch.

I was beginning to feel irritated; clearly I was failing. So I moved closer to say something to her. At the same time, the woman sitting next to Erin also leaned in. As our eyes met, I saw a horrified look on this stranger's face. Instantly a chill shot through me: *The shoulder I had been rubbing wasn't my wife's. It belonged to the woman sitting next to her!* Erin and I laugh about it to this day, but we didn't laugh that day.

After I asked my bride and the middle-aged stranger to forgive me, Erin and I managed to patch things up. Ironically, as my wife and I hopped to various islands, we kept running into this woman, who was visiting Hawaii on a special trip with a friend. We got to know both women and enjoyed dinner with them a few times. Every year we still receive Christmas cards from them, and the woman still teases me, "Now remember—any time you get tired of your wife, you already hit on me once."

That's where the Fear Dance can leave you. Fortunately, you can learn how to kick up your heels and start dancing to another tune. You can break the rhythm of your Fear Dance and learn new dance steps that will restore the marriage you've always dreamed of. May I show you how?

3

Breaking the Rhythm of the Dance

CHAPTER 5

Dance Step #1:

TAKING PERSONAL RESPONSIBILITY

"You can be sure that I have heard the groans of the people of Israel,
who are now slaves to the Egyptians. I have remembered my
covenant with them. Therefore, say to the Israelites: 'I am the Lord,
and I will free you from your slavery in Egypt. I will redeem you
with mighty power and great acts of judgment.' "

EXODUS 6:5-6

AN ELDERLY, never-married woman lived all alone in an old Victorian mansion that she had inherited. When her declining health confined her to a wheelchair, she became severely depressed and almost never left her house. In earlier years she had actively served at her local church; now she went only on Sundays.

When she hinted to a nephew that thoughts of suicide had begun running through her mind, the man contacted a psychiatrist friend of his, the late Milton Erickson, and asked him to look in on his aunt the next time he visited Milwaukee. Erickson agreed and arranged to meet the woman at her home after he spoke at a conference.

The woman greeted Erickson at her door and took him on a tour of the dark mansion. All the shades had been drawn, and except for some remodeling that made the place more wheelchair accessible, Erickson thought it looked largely unchanged from how it must have appeared in the 1890s. Finally the woman showed her visitor the only room in the house that seemed to harbor life: a greenhouse nursery where she grew African violets, her pride and joy.

As the two talked amicably, Erickson said something that both startled and upset the woman. He noted admiringly her African violets and then said, "I don't think you're being a very good Christian."

The woman took offense to his comment and insisted that she considered herself a very good Christian.

"Really?" Erickson replied. "Here you are with all this money and time on your hands, and a green thumb. And it's all going to waste. Why don't you get a copy of your church membership list and then look in the latest church bulletin? You'll find announcements of births, illnesses, graduations, engagements, and marriages in there—all the happy and sad events in the lives of people in the congregation. Make a number of African violet cuttings and get them well-established. Then place them in gift pots and hire your handyman to drive you to the homes of people who are affected by these happy and sad events. Bring them a plant and your congratulations or condolences and comfort, whichever is appropriate to the situation."[1]

Then the psychiatrist left.

About twenty years later, Erickson received a newspaper clipping from *The Milwaukee Journal* headlined, "African Violet Queen Dies, Mourned by Thousands." Sometime afterward, when he told this story to his students, one of them asked, "What on earth did you tell her? Is that all you said?"

The psychiatrist thought for a moment and then replied, "It occurred to me that it was far easier to get her to grow the African violet part of her life than it would have been to weed out the depression."

What finally freed the woman from her self-imposed slavery? What brought her out of the darkness of depression and despair and into the light of contentment and joy? She tapped into a power she didn't even know she had. Erickson helped her to realize that she had to take responsibility for herself and her attitudes. When she did that, she not only found emotional healing for herself but also a place in the hearts of thousands of Milwaukeeans touched by her kindness.

And what does a spinster's story have to do with married couples who find themselves enslaved by chains of relational discord? The exodus routes that both must take run along essentially the same path, a passageway called personal responsibility.

TAKING RESPONSIBILITY

If I were to ask you how Israel escaped from Egyptian slavery, how would you respond? Would you describe the ten plagues? You'd be right. Would you talk about the leadership of Moses? You'd be right there, too. Would you focus on God's miraculous intervention? You'd get no argument from me.

The Scriptures leave no doubt that God took the lead role in freeing his people from bondage. It was God who heard the Israelites' groaning. It was God who tapped Moses for a unique ministry of liberation. It was God who rained down ten awful plagues to convince Pharaoh to let the Hebrews go. And it was God who led his children out of Egypt, guiding them with a pillar of cloud by day and a pillar of fire by night.

And yet, we need to be careful that we don't miss something important here. While God took all the steps necessary to make the Exodus possible, God's people had to act in some specific ways in order to enjoy the benefits of his work. God did not simply teleport them, *Star Trek* style, from Egypt to the Promised Land.[2]

God acted, but he also expected his people to act. Just before the Lord sent his final plague on Egypt, he instructed the Israelites through Moses to ask their neighbors for items of gold and silver. When God sent the angel of death on all the firstborn of Egypt, his chosen people escaped with their lives only because they acted in accordance with God's explicit instructions regarding the Passover (see Exodus 12:1-30). To this day, the celebration of Passover reminds us that while God stretched out his mighty hand to free the Israelites from captivity, they participated in his deliverance only when they stretched out their own hands to paint the blood of the Passover lamb on the doorposts of their homes. And when Pharaoh finally relented and urged his former slaves to leave his ravaged country, they gained their freedom only when they acted on the Lord's instructions.

What if some foolish Israelite had said, "I'm no beggar. I'm not going to ask my Egyptian neighbors for expensive gifts"? He would remain in poverty. What if some unwise descendant of Abraham had said, "I'm not going to stain my house with the filthy blood of a sacrificed lamb"? Then all the firstborn in his household would die. What if some silly Hebrew slave had decided, "I need more advance notice than this. I'm not going to travel in the dead of night"? Then the next morning he would wake up, still a slave, but this time surrounded by angry Egyptians out of their minds with grief.

To bring his people out of slavery, God did what only he could do; but if the Israelites ever wanted to breathe free air and taste the fruit of liberty, they had to do what God asked of them. Otherwise, none of his miracles and none of his promises would benefit them in the least.

In a very real sense, the Israelites found that a key to their escape from slavery—in fact, the very first one—lay in *personal responsibility*. They had to take responsibility for their own actions, not for the actions of their neighbors.

I want to suggest that this same key enables married couples to unlock the prison doors that keep them confined inside their own brand of slavery. Learning to take personal responsibility can put them on the road to a Promised Land marriage, where they can at last experience the great dreams that God himself put in their hearts.

BREAKING THE CYCLE OF THE FEAR DANCE

I'm convinced that the only way I can break the deadly cycle of the Fear Dance is to take personal responsibility for my own actions. And what does that mean? For me, it means that I stop focusing on what Erin does and instead start focusing on what I do. When I change my focus from her actions to my actions, the cycle breaks.

Taking personal responsibility means that I give up trying to achieve my self-centered dreams for my marriage. I stop trying to force my spouse to change in ways that please me. It means taking responsibility for my own emotions and actions in the real world and refusing to live in the world as I think it *should* be—a world of illegitimate and hurtful dreams. It means making sure that I don't try to force Erin into my selfish dreams, but instead strive to discover the dreams God has for my marriage. Only in this way can I break the terrible hold that the Fear Dance has over me.

Today, whenever I start to feel like a failure, I consciously take a step back in my mind and think, *Okay, I'm starting to feel like a failure. Whatever Erin is saying and however she's saying it, I'm feeling like a failure. But it's not Erin's job to make me feel successful or valuable. I am responsible for that. God has created me with value, and he has made me the steward or caretaker of what he has placed within me. I am the responsible one, and Erin is the assistant.*

I used to spend enormous amounts of time and energy in trying to change my wife. I had locked on to the idea of changing her as the key to wedded bliss. I'd think, *If I could just get her to change. If she could just be kinder in her words. If she could only point out all the good I do. If she could just kindly suggest ways I could do better.* The problem? My continual focus on Erin and what she did set me up to be dependent. And since I had no control over how she acted, I became totally helpless.

Nothing changed in our marriage until two things happened:

1. We gained insight into our unique Fear Dance.
2. We began to understand that the key to success lay in changing our focus from our partner to ourselves, from our partner's actions to our own actions.

When I started focusing on my own actions and responses and became personally responsible for my own fear button (and when Erin did the same), we saw immediate and marked improvement in our relationship.

Note that this change of focus involves *actions*. When I say that I stop focusing on Erin, I don't mean that I discount how she feels or disregard what she thinks. Rather, I mean that I stop concentrating on how she acts toward me or responds to me; instead I focus on how *I* act and respond. I can't force her to act in a way that pleases me, but *I* can act in a way that helps our marriage. While I can take personal responsibility for what I do, I can't take responsibility for what she does. And so in this way I take the focus off of her and place it on me.

Of course, we still needed to learn how to better process our conflicts. It's one thing to stop gyrating to the raucous strains of the Fear Dance; it's quite another to learn some new dance steps designed to help your dreams come true. But the big breakthrough came for Erin and me when both of us started taking personal responsibility for our own fear buttons. Our marriage satisfaction shot up through the roof when we finally stopped worrying about what the other person might do or ought to do. After one early conflict that we defused through taking personal responsibility, I remember sitting at the table, strumming my fingers and thinking, *Why didn't we just do this every time?*

A SURE WAY TO FAIL

I can't overstate the importance of breaking the power of the Fear Dance by taking personal responsibility for your own actions. You *cannot* break the cycle, you *cannot* stop the dance, unless you first become willing to focus on yourself and your own actions. Without taking personal responsibility for your own button, you're going to stay a slave to hurt, bitterness. You'll be stuck in a marriage that is far less than what you desire in your best dreams.

Do you recall the figure I quoted earlier about how our marriage intensives have achieved more than a 90 percent success rate with couples in distress? Do you know why the other 10 percent don't make it? In virtually every case, the husbands and wives who wind up in divorce court refuse to stop focusing on their spouse. These couples get so locked into the old paradigm that they just can't let go. Either they don't trust God to do what only he can do, or they don't trust their partner to do what only he or she can do. One or both partners think, *I have to continue to focus on this person. I have to be concerned about him or her, to worry about what he or she is doing or not doing.* So they maintain an external focus and continue to zero in on their spouse.

You know what happens? Nothing. Nothing changes in their relationship. So they stay in slavery. And before long, one or both file for divorce.

At the Smalley Marriage Institute we warn each of our clients not to consider our counseling intensives a cure-all. We see them as a tool to help couples get "unstuck." We envision these clients trapped in quicksand, sinking by the side of the road. Our job is to help get them out of the muck and back on the road. We send them home with a follow-up plan, including some directions for getting connected to a small group. But if a husband and wife refuse to take personal responsibility and if they neglect to follow up on anything, our program won't work for them. And they'll land in the miserable 10 percent who split up.

RESPONSIBILITY IS NOT THE SAME AS INDIVIDUALISM

No one has to remain bound or controlled by the Fear Dance. Even though the dance is an iron-fisted slave master, it retains its power over us only when we allow ourselves to remain its servants. You and I can escape its sinister power when we choose to say, "I'm not going to do this anymore. I'm not going to try to get you to change so that I can feel good. I can focus on myself and how I respond, and then work things out with God."

Some people make a crucial mistake at this point. They confuse personal responsibility with individualism. Hear me clearly: I do *not* advocate trying to find solutions to your marital problems on your own. Here's the right paradigm for any relationship: "Although I am 100 percent responsible for the value that God has placed within me, I cannot on my own find happiness apart from God. I will never find complete satisfaction in my wife, my children, my work, money, or possessions. God, not my partner, is my source of fulfillment. God, not my spouse, is my source of satisfaction."

If at any time Erin seems unwilling to work through this process, I can still be very assertive in helping her to understand what she can do as my assistant—and she *can* do many things to help me with my Fear button. I've learned to be clear about those things. I can say to her, "When you sit down and approach me in a very calm, loving, honoring way, I feel so successful. When you point out the things I need to do better, it helps when you remind me of the grand scheme of things and say, 'We're doing really well. We just need to tinker a little with this thing.' "

It feels wonderful when Erin "cooperates." But how do I respond when she doesn't? Do I crumble? No. I may stand up and say, "Hold on. What you're saying is not okay. And the way you're treating me right now is not okay." Or I might call a timeout. Or perhaps I'll silently tell God, "You know what? Right now, God, I'm feeling like a failure. I know that I'm not. I know that I do a lot of things well in my marriage. But right now, this thing is hitting me."

I might even say something to Erin like this: "You know my issue. And right now, from the way we're talking, I feel like a total failure." Often when she hears that, she will attend to me, right then and there. And we'll immediately get back on track.

Sometimes, however, she does the reverse. "Right now," she may declare, "I feel really invalidated." And then, on a good day,

I try to validate her. But here's the point: *Even if I don't validate her or she doesn't encourage me, we're both still personally responsible for how we react.*

I wish I could say that because we've mastered this key, we have left behind our Fear Dance for good. But that would be a lie. At times we're great at taking personal responsibility; at other times we fail at it. Sometimes I get fully engaged in the cycle and try to get Erin to waltz, but she refuses. At other times she wants to rumba, and I decline. We both ought to take personal responsibility at all times—but either one of us can break the cycle, at any time, if just one of us refuses to do the destructive dance.

> **PROMISED LAND TIP**
> Accept the fact that you are 100 percent responsible for yourself, your buttons, and how you react when your buttons get pushed.

That's good news! And yet, initially at least, that very break often causes a problem.

ADJUSTING TO FREEDOM

An interesting phenomenon occurs almost every time we guide a couple through a marriage intensive at the Smalley Marriage Institute. When we write up on the board the couple's unique Fear Dance, invariably the husband and wife tell us they feel incredibly heard and validated. You can almost see new insight flowing into their brains. It's a very powerful moment.

We break for lunch, and when we return, we explain how to shatter the old cycle through personal responsibility. This whole section of the intensive often feels something like the parting of the Red Sea—a series of profound "Aha!" moments. Most couples seem really energized by the end of the day and go back to their hotels for the evening saying, "Whew! Now we know why we've been struggling. It makes sense. We can *do* this!" We hear an enormous amount of sighing and see a great deal of hope.

But nearly all of the participants tell us the next day, "You know, we almost didn't come back."

Why? What prompts such a stark reversal? And why does it happen almost 100 percent of the time?

It happens because although we encouraged husbands and wives to stop doing what wasn't working, we hadn't yet given them anything to replace it. We suggested what they *shouldn't* do but hadn't yet recommended what they *ought* to do. In a sense, they felt as if we took away their identity but failed to give them a new one.

At this stage of the intensive, most couples feel anxious and uncertain and deeply vulnerable. A good number feel far more than frustrated; in fact, they're often really ticked off at us. That's why we usually begin the next morning's session with an announcement. "You might feel very frustrated with us right now," we tell them. "It may seem to you as if we've cut off your hands but insist that you clap. And you're saying, 'We can't!' We want you to know that it's okay to feel that way because you've just entered the wilderness. The wilderness is an uncertain time, but it's also a place where you can learn some new, healthy dance steps to replace your old, destructive ones."

GROUSING IN THE DESERT

The wilderness may be necessary, but it's never comfortable. What most couples experience when they enter the wilderness closely mirrors the emotional turmoil of the ancient Israelites after their exodus from Egypt.

Try to imagine even a little of what God's people endured on their way out of bondage. For something close to half a millennium they and their ancestors had languished in forced servitude. No Hebrew could remember what it felt like to live free. Parents, grandparents, and great-grandparents all had grown up in slavery. It was all any of them knew.

Then one day the cruel Pharaoh had had enough and finally decided to let the people go. On the night of the Passover feast, after the Israelites had marked their doorposts with the blood of the Passover lamb, they were free! All of these Israelites—probably two million strong—picked up whatever possessions they could carry and marched out into the desert. To where? They are not told.

Had you been among their number, how do you think you would have felt? Uncertain? Confused? Elated at winning your freedom, yet frightened by the great unknown ahead?

When you consider the Exodus from this perspective, perhaps it doesn't seem quite so surprising that the Israelites frequently balked at their new life as free sons and daughters of Abraham. They didn't really know their leader, Moses; they had only just learned the covenant name of their God, Yahweh. So whenever things got a little dicey, no wonder their minds flew directly back to what they knew in Egypt. And their thoughts certainly did return to the land of the pyramids, forcefully and often:

> Then they turned against Moses and complained, "Why did you bring us out here to die in the wilderness? Weren't there enough graves for us in Egypt? Why did you make us leave? Didn't we tell you to leave us alone while we were still in Egypt? Our Egyptian slavery was far better than dying out here in the wilderness!" (Exodus 14:11-12)

> There, too, the whole community of Israel spoke bitterly against Moses and Aaron. "Oh, that we were back in Egypt," they moaned. "It would have been better if the Lord had killed us there! At least there we had plenty to eat. But now you have brought us into this desert to starve us to death." (Exodus 16:2-3)

In some ways, such griping and complaining boggles my mind. The Bible paints a clear image of slavery—and it isn't pretty. The Israelites had slave masters who oppressed them with forced labor, taskmasters who worked them ruthlessly and made their lives bitter. Pharaoh had cruelly ordered the Hebrews to kill all their baby boys. The people felt miserable. Yet many of these freed slaves constantly thought of returning to Egypt, where they would certainly die in harsh slavery. Why?

The reason, I think, is that it took time for them to get rid of their slave mentality. They'd always been slaves, and they didn't know anything else. They said to each other, "Better a slave than a . . . what? I don't even know the alternative."

The Israelites felt trapped between the misery of slavery and the uncertainty of an unknown future. They and their ancestors had been called slaves for centuries, and in that time they had become completely dependent on the Egyptians. Their slavery defined them. Slavery had become routine—it felt familiar, normal. They had adapted to it. Although they didn't like the pain of slavery, they had stayed alive through it. That's why they felt a constant tug to return to Egypt. *Anything* felt better to them than the uncertainty of what might lie ahead. For the Israelites, the wilderness represented uncharted territory and a strange (and therefore frightening) future.

In much the same way, married couples who escape relational slavery through learning to take personal responsibility and enter the wilderness, all experience their own kind of uncertainty and fear.

A TIME OF UNCERTAINTY

Most couples feel elated after successfully identifying their Fear Dance and seeing how they can break its rhythm. But after their joy subsides, they get more than a little nervous.

"Well, that makes sense here," they say, pointing to their charted Fear Dance. But then they point to a graphic of the Promised Land and say, "How will *this* happen?" They feel enormous uncertainty. And it's easy to see why. The moment they stop focusing on what the other person does, they feel terribly at risk. Their Fear Dance is the only system they know, and it's being taken away. What will replace it? They don't know.

Besides, there's truth to what they say. They're right when they claim, "If my spouse would just stop being harsh, that would be wonderful." Sure, it would be wonderful. Why would I deny it? But the painful truth is, people don't normally stop negative behavior just because we'd like them to. And we already know what happens over the long

haul when we insist on focusing on the other person's actions and refuse to take personal responsibility for our own actions.

The hallmark of entering the wilderness stage is a terrible feeling of uncertainty. Couples in this stage typically feel naked; we call it the Adam and Eve Effect. Just as Adam and Eve hid from God after they realized they were naked, so couples who have exposed their Fear Dance feel emotionally naked and vulnerable.

When couples first began this process, they nurtured the hope that something better lies ahead of them—a beautiful dream, a Promised Land, maybe—but they're painfully aware they haven't yet arrived. At the same time, they know they've moved out of Egypt—and even though it had become an undesirable or even bitter place, at least it was a place they knew.

And they think, *What now?*

THE CRUCIAL ROLE OF IDENTITY

We can't understand this unnerving feeling of uncertainty without taking into account the crucial role of *identity*. Humans have a deep need for connection, to be identified with others like themselves. Even nonconformists tend to hang around other nonconformists, all of whom look and talk a good deal alike. Our self-identity shapes much of how we function.

It took the Israelites many years before they stopped thinking of themselves as slaves. They could tolerate the physical pain of slavery better than they could the emotional pain of an uncertain identity.

Many couples do something very similar. They construct their identity around the elements of an unhealthy relationship, and even though that union hurts or at least disappoints, they prefer its unhealthiness to a loss of identity. Without that identity, they feel alone. Most of us define ourselves at least partly by our experiences. Someone may say, "I'm a mother" or "I grew up during the Depression" or "I'm a cancer survivor" or "I'm an adult child of an alcoholic." To some degree, our experiences define us.

When married couples become enslaved, their Fear Dance defines them. While they don't like the pain it causes, over time the dance comes to feel normal, routine, predictable—even safe. Their coping strategies, however unhealthy, are actually attempts at keeping the marriage alive.

Such couples fear breaking the dance, therefore, because the dance feels like *them*. It defines them. They are slaves to it. Once they do attempt to break it by taking personal responsibility, they feel anxious and uncertain. Who are they now, if the dance no longer defines them? They live no longer in Egypt, but they haven't arrived in the Promised Land either. They exist somewhere in between, in a kind of relational limbo.

Couples who enter the wilderness stage must understand that even though they hated slavery and despised the unhealthy aspects of their relationship, their Fear Dance still defined who they were. In a very real sense, it became their identity. And when that identity gets taken away, terrific uncertainty results—along with a desire to return to more familiar days of slavery.

COMBATING THE DEATH STAR

George Lucas made movie history (and untold millions of dollars) when he created the Star Wars universe. His space-opera films have deposited dozens of terms and memorable characters into the vault of pop culture: Darth Vader, Luke Skywalker, R2-D2, the Force, and the dark side.

For viewers addicted to gee-whiz technology and special effects, one creation probably stands out: the Death Star. This gargantuan weapon of mass destruction could vaporize whole planets with a single blast of focused energy. It boasted impressive defensive systems, too, including laser cannons, an invisible energy shield, and a mighty tractor beam that could draw fleeing ships back into its behemoth interior.

That tractor beam has become for me a potent metaphor of the power of the Fear Dance. The dance exerts a strong pull on a couple, trying to get them to return to the very thing that held them captive. When they try to flee, the Death Star tractor beam locks on to them and tries to drag them back into captivity.

Don't care for that metaphor? Then consider what science has to say. Systems theory states that every system tries to return to its original condition. Systems have a unique tendency to pull back, to keep everything from alteration. They fight change. A couple's Fear Dance has become its system, and that system powerfully resists change. The system wants to stay as it was. If it had a favorite word in the dictionary, that word would be *homeostasis*. Homeostasis is "a relatively stable state of equilibrium or a tendency toward such a state between the different but interdependent elements or groups of elements of an organism, population, or group."[3]

Couples who desire to change the way their "system" works will always have to work against homeostasis. They must face and overcome a relational inertia that wants to keep them just where they are.

Don't underestimate the power of the Death Star . . . er, the Fear Dance! Your old system is constantly pulling you to return to old patterns. If you want to escape its pull, you'll have to endure some discomfort. Because the truth is, the old system did offer a certain level of comfort. In an unhealthy sort of way, it actually "worked."

A FUNCTIONALLY DYSFUNCTIONAL WAY OF LIVING

Under the old system, when a spouse pushed our button, we coped in ways that ultimately proved unhealthy for the relationship. Not everything we did could be termed unhealthy, but what kept us stuck was our unhealthy way of coping.

Yet this unhealthy dance became functional; it kept us together and allowed us to move around each other (warily) in a circle. We term this kind of relationship *functionally dysfunctional*. While it's very *functional*—it "works" in the sense that it keeps us together—it's very *dys*functional—it causes pain, sometimes tremendous pain, and warps the relationship. Every one of the unhealthy reactions we've identified can be labeled dysfunctional: withdrawal, escalation, negative beliefs, belittling, and so forth. Eventually the dance makes us dependent on our partner for our happiness and fulfillment. And there's something functionally dysfunctional about such a dependency.

God created us to depend on him, and as human beings we naturally gravitate toward being dependent. The problem is, such dependency was designed and reserved for God alone, not for our spouses. So although the dance "worked," it cannot bring us to where we want to be.

Do you want to settle down in the Promised Land and enjoy everything that God meant your marriage to provide? Do you want to enjoy the marriage of your dreams? If so, these faulty systems and unhealthy reactions and dysfunctional ways of doing things *will not* work. I usually tell my clients, "I'm not telling you not to do them, but I am saying that if you do them, you'll never reach the Promised Land. The system you've been using is perfect for getting the results you've been getting. So if you want different results, you have to change your system. It's a choice, and the DNA of relationships reminds us that you are made with the capacity to choose."

And such a choice is bound to cause some real discomfort.

UNCOMFORTABLE BUT WORTH IT

How different would the landscape of our faith look today if the Israelites had given in to their discomfort in the wilderness and returned to Egypt! Would God ever have blessed us with such heroes of the faith as Samuel, Deborah, David, Ruth, Isaiah, Abigail, Daniel, or Esther?

Nobody likes the feelings of insecurity or uncertainty, yet such feelings are unavoidable when you take personal responsibility and enter the wilderness. And don't forget the sadness or misery you felt while still in Egypt! It's that discomfort that prompted you to move in the first place. Don't forget it! That very unhappiness and discontent can help pave the way for your exit from slavery.

I know it's uncomfortable to feel the loss of your sense of identity. I know it's hard to give up something known (no matter how painful) for something unknown (no matter how promising). I know, because I felt the same way.

When Erin and I finally identified our Fear Dance and realized that we could break its power through taking personal responsibility, I felt very uncomfortable, very threatened, very nervous about letting the old system go. It felt so hard and painful. Why? Because it meant giving up what little control I thought I had. It meant trusting my wife. I felt very insecure in leaving Egypt. I didn't know for sure what my wife was going to do.

But may I tell you what happened? When Erin and I made our decision to break the cycle and stop our Fear Dance—despite our insecurity—God did a far greater work in our lives than anything I could ever have dreamed, let alone manufactured. I had been passionately committed to changing my wife according to my own (flawed) vision . . . and then God stepped in and changed both of us in ways impossible to imagine.

I've had the privilege of watching my wife learn to validate herself through Christ. She doesn't need people to validate her now. She likes it when people value her, and she feels blessed and honored when others validate her. But she no longer turns to people to bring her fulfillment. I've never felt more freedom in life because I know that people cannot help me to ultimately feel successful. When I start to feel as if I've failed, I turn it over to Christ. I offer my pain and agony to him. I now understand that I need to stop trying to manipulate others so that I can feel successful. Erin and I both still struggle with our fear buttons. We both fall back into our Fear Dance. We both still make poor choices from time to time. But the difference is that we now have the insight and understanding that it's not the other person's job to give us what we want. Even after falling back into the dysfunctional dance, we can always get out by taking personal responsibility and offering the issue to God.

And God wants to step into your situation in similar ways.

STAYING THE COURSE

A recent survey polled seriously distressed couples, all of whom had been separated or on the brink of divorce. Yet these couples kept at it. They resisted the urge to return to Egypt—and they reaped a huge reward for it. Do you know that a full 80 percent of these couples reported a level of increased satisfaction in their relationship, simply by persevering?[4] In a wilderness stage of their marriage, with all the uncertainty and fear that it entails, they resisted their inward compulsions to dissolve the marriage or to return to the way things used to be. And what happened? They faced difficulties, but they persevered. And the couples who stayed the course reaped the benefits of their decision. That's not to say that they will not face other difficulties, but these happy couples earned the right to say, "Wow, we made it through. And it's better on this side."

You can say the same thing.

When you feel the tug of the Death Star calling you back to its familiar system, ask yourself, Is it *really* better back in Egypt? Of course not. Does the wilderness look more barren than the land of the pharaohs? I dare say it does. But God isn't calling you to the wilderness as a place to settle down and live. He's calling you out of Egypt and into the wilderness so that in that transitional place he can equip you with the skills that will make your stay in the Promised Land productive, fulfilling, and sweet.

So don't listen to the voices calling you back to Egypt. So many men and women who listen to those voices file for divorce or return to Egypt—and find it far worse than they remembered. Several studies in the past few years reveal that a very high percentage of those who divorce, just a few months later wish they had never dissolved the marriage.[5] But by then it was too late.

Entering the wilderness, where we learn new skills to help us fulfill our marital dreams and fully enjoy the Promised Land, requires that we deal with uncertainty. This is crucial to understand because many of us want to move too quickly into the Promised Land. We want to jump from misery to ideal, from nightmare to dream, without an in-between time of preparation—but that will only short-circuit the process.

In the wilderness, your marriage develops, and your relationship with your spouse grows stronger. Just because you've left slavery in Egypt doesn't mean that you've left all your problems behind! The wilderness has its own set of challenges, especially since it represents brand-new territory.

Oh, but it's worth it! Your time spent in the wilderness, learning and acquiring new dance steps, will hasten your arrival in the Promised Land and make your life there full and satisfying. But to reach that "land flowing with milk and honey," you have to be willing to live with some uncertainty. Don't be among the 10 percent who resume their Fear Dance! That road leads only to marital death. And why choose death when you can have life?

YOU'VE GOT TO LAUGH

While everyone finds it tough to live with uncertainty, it's certainly not impossible. You did it when you first got married, didn't you? You ran into any number of unexpected situations and yet came out fine. So did I.

I ran into my first challenge literally an hour into our marriage. Erin and I were waiting at the airport to catch our flight to Hawaii, both of us feeling nervous. Everything was so new and unfamiliar. A pleasant kind of tension filled the air.

When the airline personnel called our flight, I stood up, reached my hand into a carry-on bag to retrieve our tickets—and something fell out on the ground. I recognized it instantly.

The night before, my friends had given me a bachelor party. One of the guys, apparently trying to be funny, bought me a thoroughly disgusting bachelor gift—disturbing, strange, and extraordinarily sexual. I had tried to hide the thing under the torn gift wrapping, hoping that it would get tossed out with the trash at the end of the night. I didn't want Erin to see it; if I showed up with this article, I was sure she'd think me a complete sicko. But the guys had apparently recovered the item and had stuffed it into my carry-on bag.

So, there I was in the crowded airport, and this *thing* falls to the ground. Instantly Erin looked at me as if to say, *What is that?* You could almost see her mind racing, trying to understand if she'd married a pervert. At the same time, I began pushing her back, thinking that if I could just move away from the item fast enough, no one would know I had dropped it.

We had almost made good on our escape when a man some distance away yelled out, "Hey, buddy! You dropped something!" He couldn't identify the object from his vantage point, but he could see that something had fallen out of my bag. Immediately everyone turned to look. The crowd saw the item, looked at me, looked back at the item, and then glared at me. Some observers looked shocked and confused, while others started to cover the eyes of their children.

I reached for my wife's hand of support and comfort . . . and grabbed air. She had vanished down the jetway to board the plane. I stood there mute and all alone. Moms picked up their kids and moved them away from me. They really did!

With no better idea what to do, I decided to act as if such an event happened to me every day. I puffed out my chest, walked over to the item, grabbed it, and popped it into my bag. Then I fled down the tunnel.

I felt completely dejected when I finally took my seat. Erin laughed uproariously but swore that she would never leave me like that again.

The item has had a long life with us, but never in its intended role. One time Erin stuffed the thing into my jacket so that when I put on my clothes I felt this foreign object and wondered, *Hey, what's in here?* In return I once hid it in her purse so that it could surprise her at especially inopportune moments. Through the years the article has given us a lot of laughs.

You know what? I think that's the best way to handle unfamiliar territory and uncertain times. Learn to laugh! It's surely a lot better than crying.

TAP INTO THE POWER

Do you want the key to interrupting the Fear Dance for your own marriage? Do you long to escape slavery? Do you want to start seeing your greatest dreams for your marriage come true? If so, then take personal responsibility for how you react when your spouse pushes your button. Focus on you and your actions, not on what he or she does or says. Remember, *you* are responsible for your actions, and no one else.

Why would you choose to remain powerless any longer? Why would you give someone else the ability to keep you in chains of dissatisfaction and resentment when God has given you the power to walk free into the sunshine? Why would you let living nightmares terrorize your dearest relationship when you have the resources to chase them away with joyful dreams of a Promised Land marriage?

You already have the key that turns the lock barring your way to the marriage of your dreams. Now you just have to use it.

CHAPTER 6

Dance Step #2:

LEARNING TO FORGIVE

In accordance with your great love, forgive the sin of these people, just as you have pardoned them from the time they left Egypt until now.

NUMBERS 14:19, NIV

A WOMAN I'll call Sandy walked up to me during a break at one of our monthly marriage seminars and asked if she could tell me a special story. I said I'd be glad to hear it.

Sandy glowed as she poured out her tale. Something definitely seemed different about her.

First, she described her past. "It may not show today," she whispered, "but I grew up in a small town where the only thing to do was park at the gravel pit on weekends. My mom and dad divorced when I was ten. All I remember was one fight after the other. Dad was physically abusive, and I hated him for what he did. On the nights he got drunk, we'd all shiver in fear, hoping he'd pass out before he began to terrorize us. Mom was always so afraid to stop him from hitting us. She believed that he'd kill us if she interfered. I'd go to bed most nights wishing that my father would die and be gone forever."

Sandy found it difficult to continue her story, but she composed herself and began again. "As a result of my home life, I welcomed every opportunity that came along to get me out of the house. I could hardly wait to meet Mr. Wonderful and be whisked away on a white horse to our far-away castle. As you could imagine, I did everything possible to find him. I dated extensively, hoping to find the right boy. This way of thinking, however, led to multiple sexual experiences. I can't even remember them all. It seems as if all they wanted was my body. They didn't seem interested in loving me. Many nights I cried myself to sleep. My whole life was flawed. My home was the pits, my social life reeked, and Mr. Wonderful was nowhere to be found. I finally concluded that I was created to fail. I not only felt guilty about my behavior but also felt worthless and dirty. It felt as if leprosy covered my entire body."

But then Sandy started to glow again. "During my junior year of high school, I attended a special teen appreciation night at a nearby church. I went with a few of my friends, thinking that we could flirt with some of the boys. But what happened that night, I never could have dreamed possible. For the first time in my life I heard that someone loved me unconditionally. And it wasn't just anyone: it was the God of our universe! At first I thought, *He loves everyone? Right! God couldn't love me. I'm unlovable. God has to know what I've been doing. He must know about my family, my parents. He wouldn't love them.* I continued trying to rationalize away what I heard. *I've gone too far. I'm too soiled. My body is already showing the signs of my sickness.*"

Sandy continued to explain what happened that special night. "I can't tell you why," she said, wiping away a single tear, "but after hearing the pastor's invitation, I got up and walked down the aisle. I knelt before a small, wooden cross and listened as he explained how God loved me. I had finally found Someone."

Tears streamed down both of our faces, and I asked her if she'd like to continue. Without pause, she whispered, "That man—I don't even remember his name—shared the most wonderful story of how Christ gave his life for me. And he explained that if I invited God into my heart, the Lord would make me new again. Imagine that—me, a new person! Free from all that filth and pain I'd gathered. But I began to doubt that this could be true. I asked him to explain it again. I asked, 'Are you saying that no matter who I am, no matter what I've done, God will accept me? Will he forgive me, wash away my sins—forever? Will he make me new again?' That night I accepted Christ into my heart by praying this simple prayer: 'I don't understand, God, but if you say so, I admit I need you. I'm sorry for the way I've lived. I invite you to become master of my life. Lead me where you want. I'm yours. Thank you for what you say you're going to do. I can hardly wait to see it in my life.' "

A PERSONAL RESPONSIBILITY TO FORGIVE

We all love to hear stories of how God's forgiveness has radically changed and rescued tortured lives. This is as it should be.

But why do we let forgiveness remain solely the gift of God? Why do we let the story end there, especially when God himself doesn't want it to end there? While none of us can grant an eternal pardon to people, we can exercise human forgiveness to repair broken relationships. In fact, if we want to break the power of the Fear Dance in our lives, we have to become skilled at forgiveness, the second dance step in our new repertoire.

This dance step flows naturally out of the first one, taking personal responsibility. It's related, but different. While personal responsibility takes the dance in a wide arc, forgiveness has a narrower focus. Maybe it would help to think of it like the rumba and the danzon. The rumba is a fast-paced dance style that originated centuries ago among slaves kidnapped from their native Africa. In the last century, wealthy Cubans adapted the rumba into a slower and more elegant dance called the danzon—related to the rumba, but different.

The dance step of forgiveness follows closely on the heels of personal responsibility because we must choose to forgive a spouse who has wronged us. We do not wait to determine whether they "deserve" it, whether they've suffered enough, or whether we are feeling especially gracious today. We forgive because we see forgiveness as a matter of personal responsibility.

Many of us remain in slavery because we refuse to forgive a spouse who wronged us. How many marriages have foundered because one or both partners refused to forgive? The Bible makes it clear that every believer has a personal responsibility to forgive those who hurt him or her—and it does not exempt husbands and wives.

Jesus once told a story about a man who refused to forgive the trifling debt of a poor friend. This man had his friend thrown into prison, even though he himself had just been granted relief from an enormous debt that he had no hope of repaying. When the king who had forgiven this mountain of debt heard about the man's pettiness, the ruler reversed his decision. He had the man thrown into prison with instructions that the jailers torture him until he paid back all he owed (see Matthew 18:21-35). What a graphic story! And what point was Jesus trying to make? "This is how my heavenly Father will treat each of you," he said, "unless you forgive your brother from your heart" (Matthew 18:35, NIV).

When we refuse to forgive, we demonstrate that we have no real interest in taking personal responsibility for how we respond to a wrong done to us. By refusing to forgive, we think that we hurt the one who wounded us—but rarely is that the case. In fact, the one we most hurt is ourselves. Unforgiveness leads to a bitter spirit, and a bitter spirit languishes in a fetid prison of its own making. Remember the parable's final dire words? "In anger his master turned him over to the jailers to be tortured, until he should pay back all he owed" (Matthew 18:34, NIV).

When we refuse to forgive, we willingly stay in prison, constantly tortured by "jailers" who cause us nothing but agony. These jailers keep at their nasty work until we come up with the full amount needed for repayment. Yet the parable makes it plain that *not one* of us has the resources to even begin repaying this debt. So is there no hope? Jesus knew of only one hope, of only one key, which he named "forgiveness." No other key will turn the lock.

Forgiveness gives us the power to break the bonds of anger, rage, hatred, and vengeance, which all lead down the path of destruction. They are like toxins to the soul, with forgiveness the only cleanser.

Do you want to escape the slavery of a miserable marriage? Do you want to get free of the torture of your personal prison? Then Jesus has a word for you: Forgive your spouse. He offers you no other key.

FORGIVENESS AND MARITAL SATISFACTION

We do quite a bit of marriage research at the Smalley Marriage Institute. Some time ago we set out to discover any correlation between forgiveness and marriage satisfaction. We asked couples all kinds of questions about forgiveness, and we made an intriguing discovery. We found that *forgiveness accounts for about a third of marriage satisfaction.*

Wow! That's huge in my book. From the beginning of my career I always suspected that forgiveness played a significant role in happy marriages. I just had no idea how enormous a role it actually plays.

Some of the couples who come to the Institute arrive with terrible baggage: illicit affairs, emotional abuse, financial betrayal, you name it. It's obvious that the offended spouse hasn't yet forgiven the offender. In the early months of our ministry we mentioned forgiveness, but we didn't emphasize it. We knew we couldn't force someone to forgive another, and we also knew we had a very short time to work with these distressed couples.

These days, however, we highlight forgiveness as the second dance step in any program for improving and strengthening a marriage. We see forgiveness as a critical component to any successful relationship between a husband and a wife. Genuine forgiveness allows a couple to tear away from the grip of the Fear Dance, just as the power of God enabled the Israelites to tear away from the grip of Egyptian slavery.

PROMISED LAND TIP
Forgiveness is freeing someone from ever repaying me or making right the wrong. Forgiveness is part of personal responsibility.

Forgiveness helps me to stop focusing on my spouse and what she did and to start paying attention instead to myself and to what I can do. I can give up focusing on Erin through the act of forgiveness. When I forgive my wife, I free her from the duty of repaying me or making right the wrong (which often is impossible, just as it was impossible to pay the gargantuan debt owed to the king in Jesus' parable). When I forgive Erin, in effect I'm saying to her, "Although it would be nice to get repaid, I'm forgiving you. I'm pardoning you of all that debt." In this way, forgiveness can bring deep healing to a seriously wounded marriage.

DO WE LET THEM OFF THE HOOK?

We all have a choice to make when our spouse offends us in some way. We can refuse to forgive because of past mistakes. We can let the offense tear our most prized relationship apart. Or we can decide to forgive and allow the work of Christ to heal both of us.

When confronted with these choices, some people balk. They feel as if forgiveness somehow lets the guilty partner off the hook. And that idea turns their stomach.

This brings up an important point. Some people confuse forgiveness with acceptance of the wrong. They feel as if they're being asked to condone what should never be condoned. They think, *If I forgive my spouse, then I'm excusing what he [or she] did!*

But true forgiveness has nothing to do with condoning someone's sinful actions. It has everything to do with freeing us to move beyond the offense and gain the strength and stability available to us only through God's grace.

Forgiving also does not mean forgetting. How many times have we heard someone say "Forgive and forget!" Such a thing is next to impossible (barring serious brain injury). Humorist and caricaturist Kin Hubbard once wrote, "Nobody ever forgets where he buried a hatchet." It's true!

God did not wire our brains to completely forget painful events. Why not? Our Lord uses trials and painful experiences to help his people mature. When we believe that we can forget painful events and stuff away our hurts, we only prolong the inevitable. By stuffing hurts deep down in our inner self, we simply wait for an explosion. Like a volcano, the intense heat and pressure from past hurts build up until they finally erupt. And the hot ashes and molten lava cover everything in their path.

And anyway, why would we *want* to forget? William Meninger, who has written widely about forgiveness, said: "Forgiveness, then, is not forgetting. It is not condoning or absolving. Neither is it pretending nor something done for the sake of the offender. It is not a thing we just do by a brutal act of the will. It does not entail a loss of identity, of specialness, or of face. It does not release the offenders from obligations they may or may not recognize. An understanding of these things will go a long way towards helping people enter into the forgiveness process."[1]

TWO ROADBLOCKS TO FORGIVENESS

Even though many believers know they should forgive, this knowledge doesn't give them the ability to pull it off.

"Why can't I forgive?" they ask. "I know that God wants me to, but I just can't find the strength to go through with it."

Let's be honest. No one finds forgiveness an easy task. Yet I believe two main roadblocks cause most of our hesitancy to forgive.

The first is a *lack of responsibility to own up to our* own *fallenness.* If we cannot see our own faults and mistakes, how can we possibly move toward forgiveness in our marriage? We must first genuinely admit that we are not perfect and that we are quite capable of hurting our spouse. Remember what Jesus said: "And why worry about a speck in your friend's eye when you have a log in your own? How can you think of saying, 'Let me help you get rid of that speck in your eye,' when you can't see past the log in your own eye? Hypocrite! First get rid of the log from your own eye; then perhaps you will see well enough to deal with the speck in your friend's eye" (Matthew 7:3-5).

Second, *unresolved anger* keeps many believers from extending forgiveness to a spouse. If we refuse to let go of bitterness, rage, or hatred, we hold on to enormously destructive forces. These forces stand in direct opposition to the power of forgiveness. The two forces cannot coexist; there can be no harmony and no truce between them.

Do you recognize either of these roadblocks in your marriage? Is either of them keeping you from forgiving your husband or wife? How easy is it for you to say, "I was wrong" or "I am wrong"? When was the last time you told your spouse, "What you did made me angry" or "I feel bitter about what you said"?

Don't let either of these roadblocks stop your journey on the road to forgiveness. Your marriage can't afford the delay.

SEEKING FORGIVENESS FROM YOUR SPOUSE

No matter how mature or healthy your marriage is, you have to make forgiveness an ongoing priority. Times of hardship and emotional strain will come, but so long as the two of you remain committed to seeking forgiveness from one another, the hard times will become assets, not deficits. I recommend that you keep three things in mind when you seek forgiveness.

1. *Remember that your approach sets the tone of the conversation.* Proverbs 15:1 says, "A gentle answer turns away wrath, but harsh words stir up anger." When you make your voice soft and receptive to your partner's feelings and attitudes, you're bound to get a better hearing. Be gentle, tender, soothing, calm, temperate. I like to ask myself, *How humble am I right now? How willing am I to hear what my wife might say?* If I have rehearsed a rebuttal, I'm probably not ready. Remember what King Solomon says: "Patience can persuade a prince, and soft speech can crush strong opposition" (Proverbs 25:15). Calm speech can break down what looked like insurmountable opposition.

2. *Ask for specifics on how you hurt your spouse.* We often misdiagnose how we hurt our husband or wife. It helps to validate our partner's feelings and needs when we ask how our words or actions caused the pain. If your spouse doesn't immediately want to describe the hurt, don't force the issue. Give your spouse some time to build his or her thoughts. Sometimes you can ask questions that might help your partner to understand more clearly how you hurt him or her.

Proverbs 20:5 reminds us, "The purposes of a man's heart are deep waters, but a man of understanding draws them out" (NIV). How can these "deep waters" be drawn out? Through patience, genuine concern, and good questions.

3. *Don't focus on what your spouse did to you.* Remember, the second dance step of forgiveness grows out of the first dance step of personal responsibility. You do not control your spouse; thus you can't make him or her seek or accept forgiveness. You control only yourself and how you behave toward your husband or wife. By humbly seeking forgiveness and by acknowledging every aspect of your wrongdoing, you clean up your end of the mess. God does not hold you responsible for your spouse's sin, so by cleaning up your end, you wipe your own slate clean.

THE PROCESS OF FORGIVENESS

Forgiveness is not a onetime event; it is a process. Too often we hear some version of "If he really forgave me, then he would be over this by now!"

But that simply is not realistic. We shouldn't expect immediate healing or instant forgiveness, especially if we've done something extremely hurtful. Your spouse will not get over the hurt right away; it takes time.

The pain of some hurts never fully goes away. An event may spark an old memory, and the pain may return with it. I think this is one way in which God keeps us humble. It's hard to get overconfident about our emotional or spiritual maturity when we remember how things "used to be."

We need to dispense with the belief that once we say those magic words, "I forgive you," all pain and hurt instantly disappear. Forgiveness is a process, and only by going through it can we begin to heal.

A HELPFUL MODEL OF FORGIVENESS

How do we go about this business of forgiveness? I'd like to recommend the model developed by William Meninger because I believe it covers all the necessary bases.

Meninger insists that forgiveness lies entirely in the hands of the victim. Offenders can seek forgiveness, but they have no control over whether the victim forgives. This means that when our spouse somehow wounds or hurts us, we have to take the initiative to forgive. We cannot control how he or she might act, but we can control how we react.

You can greatly increase your ability to forgive by choosing to follow Meninger's five steps. While this is a process, it is not necessarily a linear one. That is, you may find yourself moving in and out of each level; it is a dynamic process, after all. When we forgive, we do so consciously and purposefully. We *choose* to forgive. And while genuine forgiveness certainly entails emotions and feelings, it is a choice, a deliberate act of the will, not an accident.

Stage One: Admit the Hurt

You cannot forgive anyone if you do not first admit the hurt. This might seem obvious, but it's often easier to live in denial (or forgetfulness) than to admit that something painful has happened to you. Psychologists call this the *pleasure principle*. All humans behave in ways that maximize pleasure and minimize pain. Sometimes we ignore it ("I don't really have a broken leg. I just like the way it turns at a ninety-degree angle!"). Sometimes we disguise it ("It doesn't bother me that she left me! And I'm sorry if you can't hear me clearly through this heavy mask."). Sometimes we hide it ("I'm not from a broken home! You can't prove it. And don't go snooping in that old trunk downstairs!").

Sometimes we stuff it ("Pain? What pain? I enjoy biting this bullet!"). It would take another book to describe all the defense mechanisms we use.

Sometimes we try to avoid the pain through laziness. We don't want to devote the energy necessary to deal with the issue, so we disregard it. Psychologist M. Scott Peck has called laziness the biggest sin and sees it as the major path toward unhealthy relationships.

Do you want to forgive? Then start by admitting the hurt. Admit what the pain has done in your life. How can you forgive someone if you don't acknowledge that something needs to be forgiven?

Stage Two: Remind Yourself of Your Worth

At this stage of the process, it's wise to do something for yourself that makes you feel valuable. Victims of hurt often feel worthless and powerless, and doing something specifically for yourself will help you to overcome any feelings of guilt you might feel. You must get active. If you continue to move in the same direction that made you feel guilty, what hope can you have of experiencing a positive change?

Remind yourself of what the Bible says about you as a Christian. In Christ, you are accepted. You are God's child. You are Christ's friend. You have direct access to God through the Holy Spirit. You are secure, free forever from condemnation. You cannot be separated from the love of God. Your life is hidden with Christ in God. You can find grace and mercy in time of need. You have not been given a spirit of fear, but of power, love, and a sound mind. You are significant, a branch of the true vine, a channel of Jesus' life. You are God's temple, God's coworker, God's workmanship. You can do all things in Christ who strengthens you.

All these things, and many more, are yours in Christ. Why feel guilty when you can feel incredibly precious? Why stay stuck in the dumps when you are seated with Christ in the heavenly realms?

Stage Three: Allow Yourself to Feel like a Victim
Once you admit your hurt, the natural emotion is to feel like a victim. Look for telltale signs of this stage: depression, listlessness, isolation, bitterness.

When these kinds of emotions assail us, we quite naturally want to medicate them. That's the modern way to soothe emotional pain. We take drugs, drink alcohol, eat food, anything that promises to make us feel better, if even for a moment. Remember, though, that such a strategy offers only short-lived benefits; it never lasts. And in the end you'll feel worse than you did at the beginning. Allow yourself to feel like a victim!

But some people wonder, *Is it right to allow myself to feel like a victim? That seems weak, or at least a little self-indulgent.* If you feel that way, then you'd better go talk to the psalmists and the apostles. They had no problem with expressing their status as victim.

Listen to the psalmist David: "My loved ones and friends stay away, fearing my disease. Even my own family stands at a distance. Meanwhile, my enemies lay traps for me; they make plans to ruin me. They think up treacherous deeds all day long" (Psalm 38:11-12).

Listen to the apostle Paul: "As you know, all the Christians who came here from the province of Asia have deserted me; even Phygelus and Hermogenes are gone. . . . Demas has deserted me because he loves the things of this life and has gone to Thessalonica. . . . Alexander the coppersmith has done me much harm, . . . for he fought against everything we said" (2 Timothy 1:15; 4:10, 14-15).

Even Jesus Christ himself cried out on the cross, "My God, my God, why have you forsaken me?" (Matthew 27:46).

These are not the cries of people who tried to hide or deny the fact that they were victims. They deeply felt the pain caused by others and expressed it openly and without shame. So should you.

Stage Four: Recognize Your Anger
While some people don't want to admit that they have become victims, others refuse to admit that they feel great anger over the

wrong done to them. Maybe they grew up thinking that the presence of anger meant the presence of sin. Perhaps they still think that people who get angry over a personal injury are bad people.

But anger is not bad! If it were, how could the apostle James say, "My dear brothers and sisters, be quick to listen, slow to speak, and slow to get angry" (James 1:19). He puts listening, speaking, and getting angry on the same platform—and who thinks that speaking or listening equals sin? Some things that we say may amount to sin, just as some of our angry actions may amount to sin. But anger itself is not sin.

In fact, anger can benefit us tremendously when we handle it in a healthy way. Anger motivates us to change and take action. It can provide the fuel in the process of forgiveness. It supplies the power to help us go the distance.

One of my favorite movies is *Back to the Future*. The plot centers on a young man who gets stuck in the 1950s. His time machine, a converted DeLorean, requires a huge amount of power—and it's on Empty. The only way he can get back to his own time is to tap some enormous surge of energy. A crazy scientist ultimately rigs his time machine "car" to catch a bolt of lightning. When the lightning strikes his car, it propels him into the future and back home.

Anger is like the lightning in the movie. If handled in healthy ways, anger can motivate us, energize us, and inform us that something is wrong. In and of itself, anger is a healthy emotion. It is a God-given emotion. The challenge is to use it appropriately. Rage or striking out to injure someone (emotionally or physically) is not using anger in healthy ways.

Anger shouldn't be about getting back at somebody, but rather about finding the motivation to change. When we focus our anger on vengeance, we hurt only ourselves. Vengeance will destroy us; it's like toxic waste to the soul. We sin when we hold on to our anger. When we refuse to let it go, it takes root in the deepest part of us and blocks our relationship with God and our spouse.

Positive anger lets us know something needs to be addressed, like the red warning lights in our car. When they start blinking, you'd better take notice. Pent-up anger might not cause problems right away, but one day it will erupt in ways that will hurt and injure everyone around you.

Stage Five: Find Wholeness
When you can forgive those who have hurt you—and when you do so with a willing heart, fully recognizing both the limits and the benefits of what you do—you reach a high stage of maturity and love. When you forgive someone, you do not place yourself on a pedestal above the one forgiven. You say, "Neither of us is perfect. I'm not, and neither are you. But since God has taken the first step to forgive me, I am now choosing to follow in his footsteps and, by his grace, to forgive you."

As you make this healing choice, others see the majesty and greatness of God himself reflected in you. And you become whole.

WHEN FORGIVENESS BRINGS WHOLENESS

Remember Sandy from the opening pages of this chapter? The first half of her story is good, but the second part may be even better.

Sandy explained to me how her life changed from the day that she accepted Christ and experienced his forgiveness. "I drove several times a week to that little church. Not long after I accepted Christ into my heart, I met Mrs. Winters. She became like a mom to me. It was great to finally have someone I could talk to about my deep secrets. We read the Bible together, and she taught me how to let God be my passion. In my teen years my passion had been boys and sex, but they left me with emptiness. When God filled my life, I truly started becoming a new person.

"Several years later my wildest dream started to unfold. I met a wonderful man. Chip was right there in my church, right under my nose. I couldn't have been more satisfied over the months that followed our meeting. But then my world shattered again when Chip shook me to the depth of my being. At age nineteen, he asked me to marry him. There was an explosion in my heart—a sorrowful explosion—a terrible pain ripping at my soul. I didn't know what it was, but I couldn't shake it. I prayed extensively for the sick feeling to leave, but it seemed to hang over me like a dark cloud."

Sandy agonized over the pain, and then finally one day it came to her. "Chip—Mr. Wonderful—had lived a life much different from mine. He'd never even touched a girl sexually. Chip was everything any girl could want. He was loving, kind, sensitive, and alert to my slightest feelings. What girl wouldn't want someone like him? But I couldn't allow myself to marry him. It would tarnish him, corrupt him to live with someone who had given herself to countless boys. I loved Chip so much that I couldn't do that. That night was like reliving one of my father's beatings. I physically shook as Chip and I sat on his front porch. 'I can't marry you,' I forced myself to say, 'We shouldn't see each other anymore.' I ran back to my car in tears. I hated myself for the lifestyle I'd lived during my teen years. I wished that I hadn't been born. If I hadn't, I never would have hurt Chip."

She tearfully continued, "Chip called me late that night. He pleaded with me to tell him why I wouldn't marry him. I could hear that his heart was filled with deep hurt. *How could I have let this go so far?* I asked myself. *Why did I use him for my happiness and then dump him like this?* But I couldn't tell him the real reason. If Chip knew who I really was, what I had done, he'd break up with me anyway. More than anything, I wanted Chip to remember me for what I had become. I was a new person.

"I couldn't sleep that night. All I could think about was this precious person I had hurt so deeply. But I could do nothing to reverse my past sinful way. I wanted to die. My stomach ached so intensely, I thought I was going to literally die. Curled up on my bed, I heard the most incredible sound. It was Chip's voice outside my window. I instantly reached for the lamp, hoping this wasn't a dream. It wasn't! Chip was outside, pleading for me to come out. Although it was 3:20 A.M., everything in me said *yes*. But I knew I still couldn't explain why. When I reached the front porch, we threw our arms around each other, as if to save the other from falling off a cliff. We couldn't let go.

" 'I won't go until I know why,' Chip demanded. 'I love you and want us to spend the rest of our lives together. Whatever it is, we can work it out. I know we can. Please tell me. Is it someone else? I need to know. Please.'

"I was so exhausted that I could no longer resist. 'Okay, I'll tell you,' I begged in tears, 'but please promise that you'll never show your disappointment in your eyes. I couldn't bear to know that my past is the reason we aren't together.'

"Chip was confused. 'What do you mean,' he asked hesitantly, 'your past?'

" 'I mean when you hear about my past,' I cried, 'you'll let me go. Please don't run away.' I hesitated for several minutes. Then, like an unplugged garden hose, my story rushed out all at once. I felt relieved but terrified all in the same breath. I sat there, waiting for him to respond. I'll never forget his words as long as I live.

"Chip simply said, 'Is that all? Don't you know how much I love you? I thought you had AIDS or something you didn't want me to have. I've racked my brain to try to figure out what I did that could make our life together impossible. But it sounds as if it's important to you that I understand your past. I forgive you. More important, I love you for who you are now. Besides, your past makes me want to love you all the more. I want you to look back on our life together and feel released from your past.'

"Mr. Wonderful sounded too good to be true. We held each other for what seemed to be the rest of the night. No words were exchanged, just silent relief. Was this really happening? Could he love me no matter what? I kept thinking suspiciously, *I know he's saying the right words now, but when we're married, he'll change. During our lovemaking, he'll remember my sins and use them against me. Don't be a fool. It will all come crashing down someday. I'm sure of it!*

"Chip lovingly and sensitively convinced me to marry him. He assured me that everything would be wonderful and we'd live 'happily ever after.' It all seemed like a fairy tale. On our wedding day, we stood at the same altar where I'd accepted Christ into my life years before. Standing in my white wedding gown as we exchanged rings, I reexperienced the sick feelings of being unworthy. It was as if I were trying to mix purity with filth. I wondered if I would ever forget what I'd done during my teen years. Not today, it seemed.

"As our beautiful wedding cake was being served, I kept thinking we'd soon be in our hotel room. Alone! *I can't do this*, I thought. Would the memories of those other boys come back to haunt me? I could feel myself tightening. *I won't be able to relax. Chip will surely notice my anxiety. I probably won't be able to satisfy him. Why am I doing this? It can't possibly work itself out—I just know it. Where are all these negative thoughts coming from? Is this how our sex life is going to be?* The questions haunted me.

"The hotel was less than a hundred miles from where we lived. We were there in no time. I hardly said anything on the drive down. 'I'm just exhausted from all the excitement of the wedding,' I told Chip. He seemed to believe me. If he knew the truth, he'd probably get angry. Just like my father. My stomach was in knots.

"In the hotel room, Chip could again tell that something was wrong. We were both nervous. I so badly wanted him to have a virgin. Chip deserved the best. I was secondhand merchandise. Why did he have to fall in love with me?

"With the bathroom door locked, I slipped into my new, white nightgown. Looking in the mirror, I was reminded that it should be a soiled color instead. After a long delay, I finally opened the door. Instantly those sick feelings again raced through my body. They were intense, my head was spinning—I was certain that I was going to throw up. And then it stopped, as if I had run full speed into a brick wall. As our eyes met, I felt captivated by Chip's loving gaze. He looked deep into my eyes, and I instantly felt peaceful. He delicately took my hand and led me to the edge of the bed. I had no idea what was about to happen.

"As I sat on the bed, Chip gently grasped my feet. I wanted to move, I felt so ashamed. Chip then pulled out a beautiful silver washbasin from under the bed. My anxiety level shot through the roof. But something about his eyes enabled me to trust him. With tender movements, Chip slowly dipped a monogrammed washcloth into the warm water and began stroking my feet. As he washed, he prayed words that instantly healed my heart and set me free from my past.

" 'Lord, as I wash my bride's feet,' he softly spoke, 'let her experience your forgiveness. Show her how you bury our sins in the depths of the ocean, never to be remembered again. Please, Lord, let Sandy hear that I've forgiven her. As she sits before me, she is a virgin. Lord, I love her with all my heart. Allow her to feel that purity. Thank you, Lord, that I have the high privilege of being with such a beautiful virgin. Thank you, Lord. Amen.'

"As Chip finished drying off my feet, I wept, out of control. With his tender prayer, he'd released years of pain and guilt. Instantly, my husband had stripped away all the years of guilt and shame forever. On the most wonderful night of my life, my honeymoon, I was able to lie beside my husband as a virgin. Since that day, I've felt like a new person—the kind of wife Chip deserved. The joy you see on my face started that day and has never left. God has truly blessed my life. He gave me Mr. Wonderful."

Sandy became whole and pure that night through the forgiveness of both God and her husband. That's the power of forgiveness—it creates wonderful new beginnings and fulfills awesome, Promised Land dreams.

For you, too.

CHAPTER 7

Dance Step #3:

HONORING EACH OTHER

When Pharaoh finally let the people go, God did not lead them on the road that runs through Philistine territory, even though that was the shortest way from Egypt to the Promised Land. God said, "If the people are faced with a battle, they might change their minds and return to Egypt." So God led them along a route through the wilderness toward the Red Sea.

EXODUS 13:17-18

MY UNIVERSITY professors and professional mentors taught me all kinds of healthy skills designed to help marriages and families. I received excellent training in cognitive-behavioral family systems, in effective communication tools, and in a host of other areas. I've read a lot in my field and am aware that multitudes of great books have been written on these topics. I have benefited from all of them.

But for the longest time I could not figure out the best way to teach husbands and wives these wonderful skills. So I continued to wonder: Was there an optimal order in which to learn and apply these skills? Did it matter which ones came first?

Further years of counseling experience with couples from across the United States have taught me that a definite flow to this process really does exist. There is an optimal order.

First, a husband and wife have to gain insight into their unhealthy patterns and understand how to escape from the slavery those patterns promote. Then, once they leave Egypt, they have to slow down and spend some time in the wilderness, learning and mastering a few essential relational skills. In other words, they have to follow the basic pattern pioneered by the ancient Israelites.

WHY THE LONGER ROUTE?

God could have taken Israel on the short route to the Promised Land, but he didn't. Exodus 13:17-18 explicitly tells us that the Lord avoided this more direct itinerary. Why?

For one thing, the warlike Philistines lived along this shorter route. God knew that if the Israelites had to strap on battle armor so soon after leaving Egypt, their slave identity would likely reassert itself and they would drop their spears and sprint back to the pyramids. To avoid that risk, God took his people on the scenic tour.

But I think God chose the wilderness route for a second, more profound reason. The Lord wanted to do far more than free some slaves; he wanted to prepare a free people who would follow him wholeheartedly and willingly. And in order to accomplish that, he had to teach these former slaves a new way of living. The wilderness became Israel's classroom. It's like the adage "Give a man a fish, and he'll eat for a day; teach a man to fish, and he'll eat for a lifetime." The wilderness became God's way of teaching the children of Israel to fish.

In the wilderness, God provided his people with the basics of life: water, food, shelter, and guidance. In time the people learned how to live under God's authority and how to receive and enjoy the blessings he wanted to give them. The Lord also taught the Israelites the skills they'd need in the Promised Land: crucial skills of leadership, warfare, worship, relationships, public health, and more.

In the wilderness, God's people shed their slave identity

and began to see themselves as a free people made in the image of God. And it was in the wilderness that God weaned the Israelites from dependence on the Egyptians to reliance on their Lord. Only then did they become ready to enter the Promised Land.

A TIME TO ACQUIRE SKILLS

A married couple who leaves its own Egypt likewise enters a time of preparation in the wilderness. Much as God prepared his people for life in the Promised Land, so husbands and wives can prepare by learning and practicing certain crucial skills. These skills help lessen the uncertainty and increase hope through bringing small victories.

It's not enough merely to identify and break unhealthy patterns. Learning to take personal responsibility and to forgive each other gets you moving in the right direction, but by themselves these first two dance steps just aren't enough. Something has to replace our old habits or they'll reassert themselves with a vengeance. A lesson Jesus once taught illustrates my point. "When an evil spirit leaves a person, it goes into the desert, searching for rest. But when it finds none, it says, 'I will return to the person I came from.' So it returns and finds that its former home is all swept and clean. Then the spirit finds seven other spirits more evil than itself, and they all enter the person and live there. And so that person is worse off than before" (Luke 11:24-26).

What is true in the spirit world is also true in the world of marriage. It is not enough merely to sweep away the old behavioral patterns and put things in order. If something more pure and more powerful does not enter the relationship and take up residence, the final condition of that marriage is worse than the first. Both cleansing and furnishing must take place, and in the right order. Perhaps this helps to explain why merely teaching couples better communication skills doesn't necessarily lead to successful and satisfying marriages.

What is the dance step that will help you develop pure,

healthy patterns? Learning to honor each other. If the Fear Dance rules in Egypt, then the Honor Dance reigns in the wilderness.

THE HONOR PRINCIPLE

For more than thirty years my dad has based his ministry on the concept of honor. Life goes so much better for everyone when we treat others like priceless treasures. I tell couples in our intensives, "In spite of everything you have gone through, don't forget that God made you both in his own image. I don't care what you have done to each other, you're still worthy of being treated as staggeringly valuable."

If you ever doubt your value, then consider how your heavenly Father sees you:[1]

- You may not know me, but I know everything about you (see Psalm 139:1).
- You were made in my image (see Genesis 1:27).
- In me you live and move and have your being (see Acts 17:28).
- You are my offspring (see Acts 17:28).
- I knew you even before you were conceived (see Jeremiah 1:4-5).
- I chose you when I planned creation (see Ephesians 1:11-12).
- You were not a mistake, for all your days are written in my book (see Psalm 139:16).
- I determined the exact time of your birth and where you would live (see Acts 17:26).
- You are fearfully and wonderfully made (see Psalm 139:14).
- I knit you together in your mother's womb (see Psalm 139:13).
- I brought you forth on the day you were born (see Psalm 71:6).
- You are my treasured possession (see Exodus 19:5).

Whenever I think of honor, I recall a story first published almost forty years ago in *Woman's Day* magazine.[2] In "Johnny Lingo's Eight-Cow Wife," author Patricia McGerr tells how a Pacific Islander married a plain girl named Sarita and through honor helped her become a stunning young bride.

In that part of the world, a young man seeking the hand of a young woman paid a dowry to her father in the form of cattle. A plain girl might fetch a single cow; an average girl might rate two or three cows; and a highly desirable girl might attract a dowry of four or five cows. Everyone in the islands considered shy, dour Sarita a one-cow wife. And yet Johnny Lingo, a highly successful businessman and entrepreneur, paid eight cows for the right to marry her. All his neighbors laughed at him behind his back, chortling that he had been cheated.

But Johnny knew what he was doing.

A visitor who heard this story made an appointment to see Johnny. In the course of their conversation the visitor met Sarita. He could hardly believe his eyes. "She was the most beautiful woman I have ever seen," he said. "The lift of her shoulders, the tilt of her chin, and the sparkle of her eyes all spelled a pride to which no one could deny her the right." And how did Johnny Lingo explain her remarkable transformation?

"Do you ever think," he asked, "what it must mean to a woman to know that her husband settled on the lowest price for which she can be bought? And then later, when the women talk, they boast of what their husbands paid for them. One says four cows, another maybe six. How does she feel, the woman who was sold for one or two? This could not happen to my Sarita."

"Then you did this just to make your wife happy?"

"I wanted Sarita to be happy, yes. But I wanted more than that. This is true. Many things can change a woman. Things that happen inside, things that happen outside. But the thing that matters most is what she thinks about herself. In Kiniwata, Sarita believed she was worth nothing. Now she knows that she is worth more than any other woman in the islands."

"Then you wanted—"

"I wanted to marry Sarita. I loved her and no other woman."

"But—"

"But," he finished softly, "I wanted an eight-cow wife."

I first read this story after Erin and I began dating. She didn't know yet how I felt about her, and I hadn't successfully communicated how much I cared for her. Neither of us had yet dared to say "I love you," but we had reached that awkward stage in a relationship in which both of us wondered, *Where is this going? Either it needs to develop into a friendship and nothing more, or we need to go to the next level.*

I loved the Johnny Lingo story and wanted to use it as a word picture to illustrate my feelings for Erin. One night she came right out and asked, "Where is our relationship going?"

"Well," I replied, "do you really want to know how I feel about you?"

"Yes!" she answered.

I looked deep into her eyes and said, "You are like an eight-cow woman to me."

I had been hoping for a reply like, "You romantic thing, you! I love you, too!" But instead I saw a very different expression form on my beloved's startled face: "You think I'm a *cow.* . . . You think I'm fat?"

I meant no such thing, of course. Erin ran track in college and has always remained fit. How was I to know that she had never read McGerr's story?

Sensing impending doom, I stammered and rambled and finally managed to blurt out, "No, no, wait. Hear me out." I then told her the whole story, concluding it by saying, "In the same way, I'd pay ten cows for you" (I thought I had better up the ante).

The expression on Erin's face immediately changed. Clearly, she got it. And three or four weeks later, we got engaged.

When Johnny Lingo treated Sarita as if she were worth eight cows, she became an eight-cow wife. In the same way, when we treat our spouses with the honor they deserve, they find the strength and joy to become masterpieces of God's handiwork.

Jesus told us, "Wherever your treasure is, there your heart and thoughts will also be" (Matthew 6:21). When you consider your spouse your treasure, your heart will follow—and so will your words and actions. Conversely, if you consider your spouse a piece of junk (or worse), he or she will never capture and hold your heart—and your words and actions will demonstrate the

> **PROMISED LAND TIP**
> Honor your spouse by recognizing his or her value, and then act in accordance with that value.

fact. When one spouse doesn't value the other, when that spouse isn't seen as a treasure, hardness of the heart sets in. And hardening of the heart is the kiss of death to a relationship.

THE DEATH KNELL OF LONELINESS

Dr. John Gottman, author of *The Seven Principles for Making Marriage Work* and *Why Marriages Succeed or Fail,* has extensively researched how a marriage ends up on the rocks. He calls this demise "the cascade of isolation." He has studied loneliness at length and considers it the emotion most destructive to a relationship. If loneliness sets in, the marriage dies.

Suppose a couple begins to have conflicts that the partners don't successfully work out together. Over time they start to deal with the problems apart from one another. As they get good at working out their conflicts alone, they become at risk for leading parallel lives. They coexist, but they begin to separate. And when they start to lead fully parallel lives, isolation and loneliness follow close behind.

God created us as relational beings. We long for connection. It goes against our natural craving to feel alone or isolated. Such a relationship will not last. And as loneliness spreads, divorce often enters the picture.

Consider a powerful and extended emotional word picture I received not long ago from a woman whose husband walked out of their marriage.

I was the latest and best new driver when a fairly new golfer bought me. Right away we were a special team. With me he hit the ball farther and straighter.

My golfer told everyone how special I was and how he had never played better because of me. He took me into the clubhouse after a round and continued to sing my praises. When we got home, he polished and shined me. He took me into his room between uses instead of leaving me in the garage with his other clubs. I felt so special and pampered. I tried to help turn through the shot and climb high on the backswing and follow through.

Occasionally, we hit a ball into the water or the rough, but together we won many tournaments and lots of money. Sometimes I could feel his grip tighten, or we swung too fast, and then he would not hit the ball well. On those occasions, he would become very emotional and blame me, but then he cheered up, regained his balance, and continued winning.

As we played more and more, his grip steadily tightened and he swung harder. We hit balls in all sorts of bad places. My golfer became progressively more frustrated and angry. And he blamed me every time. His attitude toward me changed. Instead of treating me with care, he would throw me angrily into the bag without my cover. Once he even threw me into the lake, only to come get me. I tried to follow his swing, but the line and tempo were off. I couldn't turn through the shot as before.

His anger grew, and he quit taking me into the clubhouse after a round or into his room at night. He even told everyone that he didn't know why he had bought me and that he had never hit well with me. I felt so insulted and hurt.

Several people suggested that my golfer should take a few lessons with a pro, but he refused, saying that there was nothing wrong with his swing. He said the problem was the crowding of the course, the weather, his headache, the noise made by the other golfers, and the stupid club—that I was too long, too stiff, too light, weighted incorrectly, and so on.

One day he exploded after a bad shot and threw me down

on the ground after hitting the cart with me. He was so angry! When we got home, he threw me into the corner of the garage. Thank goodness I had my cover on.

Finally, he didn't take me to the course anymore. The new clubs he bought to replace me soon joined me in the corner of the garage, saying that his grip was too tight for them, also, and that he swung too fast. I never made it out of that cold, dark corner of the garage.

This hurt and lonely woman went on to say, "The worst part of my marriage was that I came to a point where I actually missed being abused by my husband. As crazy as this sounds, at least when he was yelling, we had some kind of contact. I had his attention. Anything is better than feeling totally alone."[3]

Do you see now why I consider honor such a critical dance step? Couples who don't address serious marital problems eventually cease to value their spouses. They get so irritated and frustrated by their buttons getting pushed all of the time that they stop treating their partners as priceless. They see their spouses as worthless—and they treat them accordingly.

This is exactly what happened to Erin and me during the first years of our marriage. We endured so much conflict that I thought we were just one more argument away from a separation. One thing about those days stands out: Honor seemed to vanish the moment we started having marriage problems. Only after our mentors at Denver Seminary, Dr. Gary and Cary Oliver, encouraged us to begin to repair our relationship by recapturing the honor that had once flourished in our relationship, did we begin to see hope.

HONOR, BAMBOO, AND TIME

I liken honor to the Chinese bamboo tree. What's so special about bamboo? The Chinese bamboo tree does not produce much noticeable outward growth for the first four years of its life. Instead, when it enjoys the right kind of soil, water, sunlight, and weeding, all of its growth takes place underground. Observers see nothing on the surface except a little bulb and a small shoot. Doesn't sound like the perfect marriage relationship, you say? Just wait.

The Chinese bamboo tree first develops thick roots, called rhizomes. The plant limits its surface growth while its network of roots spans deep and wide, providing a firm base for massive growth. If you looked at a young Chinese bamboo tree, you might think, *That is the puniest, most pathetic tree I've ever seen. It's been several years without any noticeable growth. There must be something wrong with this tree.* You might feel tempted to dig it up. But if you tried, something amazing would happen. If you took hold of that tiny tree and pulled with all your might, nothing would happen. No matter how hard you yanked and jerked and tugged, you could not pull the tree out of the ground.

In the fifth year of growth, the Chinese bamboo plant shoots up a staggering *eighty feet.* Can you imagine? Something that had been growing without much visible progress for four years, in the next year develops into an eighty-foot tree! [4]

The same thing can happen in your marriage when you practice honoring each other. If you want a marriage that is like an eighty-foot Chinese bamboo tree, don't get discouraged when you see little external growth in your relationship. First you need internal growth. And honor is the best place to start.

Honor is so powerful, in fact, that it can also help you to finish. I learned that when I tried to run a marathon.

I had dreamed and trained for six months to complete a marathon, but by the eighteen-mile marker on the day of the race, my calves began cramping up. An alarming thought struck me when I felt an intense tingling sensation throughout my body. *I've hit the wall! This can't be happening now. I still have eight miles to go!* But with each step, my body fought my mind.

Erin found me at the next mile marker. Expecting to see me running along joyously, she first thought I had injured myself. As I explained my dilemma, all I could think about was quitting. I felt that if I had to walk the remaining distance, my dream of running a marathon had failed. But as I struggled with putting one foot ahead of the other, Erin said something I'll never forget.

"I believe in you!" she yelled.

Erin's encouragement seemed so simple: "I believe in you." I've heard her use those words many times. But at that moment, when I felt so utterly defeated, her words gave me a burst of energy.

The rest of the race looked like a scene out of a *Rocky* movie. With each agonizing step, Erin remained by my side. Some friends and family joined in the long walk. As we reached the twenty-fourth mile, however, I couldn't endure walking any longer. If I was going to finish the race, I had to start *running*. After several yards, my calves began functioning again, and I was able to jog. Finally, after 26.6 long miles, Erin and I crossed the finish line . . . together.

She believed in me!

One of the best ways to honor your spouse is to believe in his or her dreams—including legitimate dreams for your marriage. As the pressures of life intensify, sometimes the difference between going after a dream and remaining passive is having someone say, "I believe in you!"

DO IT ANYWAY

Perhaps you have just escaped from Egypt. Maybe only recently you struck the chains of slavery from your hands and feet. At this moment you may not feel like honoring your spouse. Do you want my advice?

Do it anyway.

Despite all the misery your spouse may have put you through, try to recapture a little of the enormous value that God placed in him or her. Look at your spouse as a priceless treasure. Only that kind of mind-set will set the right tone. Begin today to set the foundation of honor. Start slowly, with just a couple of practical exercises:

- Decide that your spouse's opinions, concerns, and expectations are just a little more valuable than your own.
- Make a list of all of your husband's or wife's positive characteristics and qualities. Your appreciation list will provide you with points of value. And know this: The longer your list, the stronger your marriage.

You already know what your Fear Dance looks like. Now try to discover the graceful moves of your own Promised Land Honor Dance!

CHAPTER 8

Dance Step #4:

TAKING CARE OF YOURSELF

The Lord said to Moses, "Look, I'm going to rain down food from heaven for you. The people can go out each day and pick up as much food as they need for that day."

EXODUS 16:4

I LIKE TESTS. I don't mean taking them, I mean giving them. So I'd like to begin this chapter with another little quiz. Don't worry, it should be fun—and if you find it difficult, well, then maybe you need more help than this book has to offer.

Ready? Begin.

1. **If you were about to undergo heart surgery, would you prefer**
    A. An overworked, sleep-deprived doctor who hadn't eaten in two days;
    B. A nervous, preoccupied physician who doesn't believe in delegation (and who bars nurses and other doctors from the operating room); or
    C. A well-rested, fit, trim, highly experienced surgeon who relies on and works well with a competent, well-trained staff?

2. If you were about to take a flight across the Atlantic Ocean, would you prefer

A. A hard-living, party-animal pilot suffering from a major hangover and extreme short-term memory loss;

B. A pilot and copilot team who regularly have physical struggles over control of the plane, and who both refuse to take direction from the control tower; or

C. A cockpit crew who annually rate at the top of their profession, have won numerous awards for their flying expertise, and who personally trained every Air Force One crew for the past fifteen years?

If you chose C for each of the two previous questions, congratulations! You stand a much greater chance of enjoying a long life than those who chose A or B. Oh, and one other thing: you've also endorsed the critical importance of good self-care.

STAYING HEALTHY IN THE WILDERNESS

Only those who take good care of themselves remain able to take the best care of others. Doctors who make it known that they don't get enough sleep, neglect to eat right, and scorn the assistance of others do not attract a long waiting list of patients. Pilots who drink too much, party too hard, and try to do everything on their own soon find themselves without an employer. Why? Because only those who take good care of themselves are in a position to take the best care of others.

God taught his people good self-care in the wilderness. He taught them how to care for their needs. He provided manna from heaven, but they had to gather it up and prepare it in nutritious and flavorful ways. He gave them streams and pools of water, but they had to draw the water out and devise ways to store it for the long journey. He gave them instructions for living, but they had to carefully carry them out. God wanted his people to learn how to take good care of themselves. To accomplish this, he provided all the resources they needed to remain healthy and strong. But if they neglected his instruction or thought they could devise a better way, they suffered the consequences—and if they suffered, so did their children.

S. I. McMillen many years ago wrote a classic book titled *None of These Diseases.*[1] In it he describes how God's dietary and worship instructions actually prevented Israel from succumbing to the terrible diseases suffered by the pagan nations around them. God wanted his people to take good care of themselves! He wants the same thing today.

My colleague Bob Paul, who pioneered the Smalley Marriage Institute's work on self-care, says that self-care is always in the best interest for everyone in the relationship. Always.

BUT ISN'T IT SELFISH?

Very often when we start talking about the necessity of good self-care, some people will object, "But that's selfishness! How can you say that God wants me to be selfish?"

Their question reminds me of an old saying by Mark Twain: "The difference between the right word and the almost right word is the difference between lightning and the lightning bug." *Selfishness* and *self-care* are not close to being the same

> **PROMISED LAND TIP**
> Taking good care of yourself is always best because you can't give what you don't have.

thing. The first, God condemns; the second, he commands. To get this straight—to see the enormous difference between lightning and the lightning bug—consider just three major differences between selfishness and good self-care.

1. *Selfishness is an end in itself; self-care is an end outside itself.* A selfish man focuses exclusively on himself and what he wants. A selfish woman cares about others only insofar as they can give

her what she demands. A selfish person has only one overriding concern: himself or herself. All else fades into insignificance. The world begins and ends with the selfish individual.

Good self-care, on the other hand, enables people to stay in top condition so that they can most effectively help others. Those who neglect to take care of themselves—like sleepwalking doctors and drunken pilots—put at great risk the lives entrusted to their care.

Why do you think flight attendants always tell adults that in the case of an emergency if oxygen masks were to drop from an overhead compartment, the adults should put on their own masks first before they try to put on their children's masks? Someone might think, *But that's so selfish!* In fact, it's no such thing. If a father unequipped with an oxygen mask should black out in an unexpected cabin depressurization, who would help his children to get their own masks on? Unconscious fathers and mothers cannot keep their children alive, but conscious ones can.

2. *Selfishness considers only its own needs; self-care considers the needs of others as well.* Everybody has needs, and it's not wrong to take them into consideration. Jesus did not tell people to neglect their needs or to act as if they didn't exist; in fact, he told them that "your heavenly Father already knows *all your needs,*" things like food and shelter and clothing (Matthew 6:32, emphasis added). Selfish people, however, think only of their own needs. The needs of others don't even register.

People who exercise good self-care, on the other hand, understand that they can best meet the needs of others by remaining up to the task. By taking good care of yourself, you put yourself in the best possible position to care for others. If you let yourself go, you put at risk the well-being of those you love the most.

3. *Selfishness demands to be served; self-care asks for help.* Selfish people do not ask for help; they demand to be served. Since they consider themselves the center of the universe, it only makes sense to them that the universe should make every effort to make them comfortable.

Men and women who understand the necessity of self-care take a much different approach. They realize they can't do it all, so they have no problem asking for help; yet they do not demand it as an inalienable right. As they serve others, they realize that they, too, sometimes need others to serve them. They do not demand this or insist on it, but without hesitation they ask for it.

WAS JESUS SELFISH?

Do you see the difference between selfishness and good self-care? If not, let me ask you a question. Would you call Jesus selfish? Would you call the apostle Paul selfish? If you still equate good self-care with selfishness, then you had better get prepared to label both men as selfish because both of them engaged in good self-care.

The Bible tells us that when Jesus needed some alone time with his Father, he had no problem with dismissing the crowds and heading off toward a solitary place (see Matthew 14:22-23). When he grew thirsty, he didn't hesitate to ask for a drink (see John 4:6-7; 19:28). When he grew hungry, he looked for something to eat (see Matthew 21:18-19). When the demands of a hectic schedule exhausted both him and his followers, he insisted that they all get some rest (see Mark 6:31). And he welcomed tangible help from friends (see Mark 15:40-41; Luke 8:3).

Paul also learned these lessons well. The discouraged and beat-up apostle asked a friend to come to him quickly and to bring along some personal clothing and supplies (see 2 Timothy 4:13, 21). Throughout Paul's career he asked for and received the tangible, concrete help that others were willing to give (see Acts 24:23; Philippians 2:25). And he didn't hesitate to tell his friends to practice good self-care. So he told his protégé, "Don't drink only water. You ought to drink a little wine for the sake of your stomach because you are sick so often" (1 Timothy 5:23).

Is any of this selfish? Hardly. Neither the Son of God nor the apostle of grace could finish the ministries God had given him without attending to good self-care. Paul even writes in a famous passage on marriage, "No one hates his own body but lovingly cares for it, just as Christ cares for his body, which is the church. And we are his body" (Ephesians 5:29-30). You *have* to feed and care for your own body, Paul says. Everyone must do this, even the Son of God himself. In fact, even after Jesus' death and resurrection, he continues to care for his body in the form of his church. That's not selfish, Paul says; that's how God designed things from the beginning.

A PERSON OF INCREDIBLE VALUE

In any event, it makes no sense to drain your personal resources for others while despising yourself. Every man or woman whom God ever created—and that includes you—was made in God's own image (see Genesis 1:27). That means you are a person of incredible value, just as much as are your children or your spouse or your neighbor or your friend.

So, as people made in the image of God, and therefore people of incredible value, do your children and spouse and neighbors and friends deserve to be treated well? Certainly. And so do you.

If you have placed your faith in Jesus Christ, then you have been given even greater value, for the blood of Christ has been shed so that you might have eternal life. The apostle Peter says to you, "For you know that God paid a ransom to save you from the empty life you inherited from your ancestors. And the ransom he paid was not mere gold or silver. He paid for you with the precious lifeblood of Christ, the sinless, spotless Lamb of God. God chose him for this purpose long before the world began, but now in these final days, he was sent to the earth for all to see. And he did this for you" (1 Peter 1:18-20). Would God spill the precious blood of Christ for someone he didn't consider precious?

Beyond that, if you belong to Christ, then even now God is at work within you so that you increasingly mirror the goodness and glory of Christ. Paul says that "all of us have had that veil removed so that we can be mirrors that brightly reflect the glory of the Lord. And as the Spirit of the Lord works within us, we become more and more like him and reflect his glory even more" (2 Corinthians 3:18).

Would you treat Christ poorly? Would you neglect him? If not, then why would you neglect or treat poorly someone who increasingly mirrors his likeness—someone like yourself?

And it gets even better! Right now, at this very moment, God himself has taken up residence in your physical body. The Bible calls your body "the temple of the Holy Spirit" (1 Corinthians 6:19). You might wonder, does it make any difference to God how you treat his temple? You'd better believe it does! Paul writes to the church, "God will bring ruin upon anyone who ruins this temple. For God's temple is holy, and you Christians are that temple" (1 Corinthians 3:17).

Does that put a different spin on the importance of good self-care for you? It should! Neglect has a way of destroying the temple that is your body—and God takes such a tragic event *seriously*.

So should you.

FOUR KEY AREAS OF SELF-CARE

Good self-care recognizes that if I'm 100 percent responsible for myself, then I have to learn how to honor and manage myself. I have to keep on top of how I'm doing mentally, physically, spiritually, and emotionally. I have to monitor these four areas constantly.

Scripture itself points out the crucial nature of these four areas of self-care. A famous verse about Christ's adolescent years says that "Jesus grew in wisdom and stature, and in favor with God and men" (Luke 2:52, NIV). The Lord's growth in "wisdom" parallels the mental component of self-care; his growth in "stature" speaks to the importance of the physical dimension; "in favor with God" points to the spiritual component; and "in favor with men" declares his social development, which naturally depends in great part on emotional maturity. Let's take a brief look at each of the four areas.

The Mental Component of Good Self-Care

Ask yourself, "What am I doing mentally to stay healthy? Am I studying, gaining knowledge?"

Some people do not grow in their faith because they neglect the intellectual aspect of their relationship with God. They fail to realize that real growth in grace does not come without considerable mental effort. Have you ever noted how often God in his Word uses terms like *mind* and *thoughts* and *meditation* and *ponder*? Such words play a prominent role in the book of Romans, considered by many experts to be the most theologically important work in the New Testament. Yet you cannot gain the greatest benefit possible from that book without first committing yourself to some strenuous thinking.

Recent scientific research shows that keeping your brain active—doing crossword puzzles, taking a different route to work, eating with your left hand instead of your right, changing your routine in even small ways—helps to build mental muscle and decreases your chances in later years of succumbing to serious brain disorders such as dementia. Books such as *Keep Your Brain Alive* by Lawrence Katz and Manning Rubin and *Brain Candy* by Thedore Lidsky and Jay Schneider give great ideas for how to exercise your mind.[2]

The Physical Component of Good Self-Care

Ask yourself, "Physically, am I taking care of my body? Am I getting enough exercise? Am I eating right? Am I getting enough sleep? Am I avoiding harmful addictions?"

While many ancient religious groups such as the Gnostics considered the body an unfortunate thing and all things material evil, Christianity never adopted such a viewpoint. While the Christian faith certainly ranks most spiritual concerns over merely temporal ones, it never teaches that the body is to be disregarded or neglected. So the apostle Paul can write that physical exercise has value (see 1 Timothy 4:8). Paul tells us that we Christians do not belong to ourselves but to God. And since our bodies have become temples for the Holy Spirit, the apostle says explicitly, "So you must honor God with your body" (1 Corinthians 6:20).

How do you honor God with your body? One thing's for sure: You do not honor God by giving out so much that you feel constantly run down, listless, or weary. You do not honor God by attending to everyone else's physical needs but your own. You do not honor God by trying to "get by" on three hours of sleep so that the rest of the family can get eight.

"Honor God with your body," Paul says. What does that mean for you?

The Spiritual Component of Good Self-Care

Ask yourself, "Spiritually, what does caring for myself look like? Is it having devotions, praying, or something else? How regularly do I meet with other believers for mutual encouragement and instruction? Can I say that I know God better today than I did a year ago?"

As I've said, you and I were made for a loving, dependent relationship with God. Since we are made in God's image and God is Spirit (see John 4:24), you and I are essentially spiritual beings. God calls on us to nurture and develop this spiritual aspect of our lives.

The apostle Peter says it like this: "Grow in the grace and knowledge of our Lord and Savior Jesus Christ" (2 Peter 3:18, NIV). You grow in grace by spending time with God, meditating on his Word, interacting with other Christians in a regular and significant way, reaching out to others, lifting your heart in worship. Those who shortchange their own spiritual growth out of a flawed desire to attend to the needs of others end up shortchanging everyone.

The Emotional Component of Good Self-Care

Ask yourself, "How am I attending to my emotional needs? Do I even know what they are? Can I usually identify my emotions in various situations? Do I know what to do when I feel sad or angry or frightened or happy?"

Many of us do the poorest job of monitoring ourselves in the realm of the emotions. I'm no exception. Think of your emotions like the dashboard of your car. Suppose that while you're driving, you see the engine light blinking. You think, *Hmm, I wonder what that could be? Oh well, I'm sure it's okay.* So you keep driving, even though the light continues to blink. You drive mile after mile—and finally the engine blows.

We should treat our emotions as invaluable internal feedback. Our emotions function like a first-alert system, a primary internal response system. A lot of times we simply don't pay enough attention to what our emotions tell us.

And how do we benefit when we monitor our emotions? First, we're more inclined to recognize things that we like. We learn more about ourselves and so can do a better job of self-care. Second, we're able to help others by communicating how much we appreciate the positive things they do.

> **PROMISED LAND TIP**
> Caring for yourself is your God-appointed responsibility leading toward being filled mentally, physically, spiritually, and emotionally.

By making it a habit to check your emotional dashboard, you more quickly become aware when your fear buttons get pushed. You learn to treat your feelings as feedback and ask yourself, "What's going on right now? What just happened? Why am I feeling this way? Is there an expectation that wasn't met? Was my button being pushed? If it is, then what do I want to do about it?"

In *Why Marriages Succeed or Fail*, Dr. John Gottman teaches couples how to do something he calls "self-soothing." I don't like the term, but his concept can do wonders. When I sense my button is getting pushed, I can begin to respond by soothing myself. I can say, "You know what? I'm starting to feel like a failure. Something's not happening right. Relax. It's okay. I'm really not a failure in the big scheme of things." Such self-talk gets me in a different spot so I can choose more productively how I want to respond to my wife. Do I want to defend myself? Do I want to argue with her? Or do I choose to listen to her because I know that makes her feel truly valuable? I love my wife and I want to honor her—so I can choose to listen to her.

Last night, Erin made a negative comment about something I had done. Almost instantly I felt my body react. My heart rate shot up, and I sensed feelings of frustration, irritation, and discouragement. When I recognized those negative emotions kicking in, I saw my cue to tell myself, "Okay, my button's been pushed." So I said, "Hey, Erin, help me to understand this. It sounds like that really frustrated you."

Don't misunderstand; even to say that much pained me deeply. I desperately wanted to show Erin briefcases full of graphs and charts on what I'd done and how she did not speak the truth. But I stopped myself. I thought, *You know what? I'm okay. I'm really not a failure.* Then I could work through the problem in a constructive way and ultimately choose to serve my wife.

Of course, I realized that Erin was doing some potentially unhealthy things. Perhaps she was angling for validation. But so what? Erin doesn't control me; I'm in charge of myself. So despite what my insecure self wanted to do, I chose to listen to my wife, validate her feelings, and serve her. And within moments, the incident came to an end.

THE SAD RESULTS OF SELF-NEGLECT

I probably don't have to detail what can happen when you neglect self-care, but as a final warning shot, let me at least tell you a sob story—my own.

In college I followed the pattern of untold millions of students and frequently didn't give much attention to self-care. My eating habits didn't exactly keep my temple looking spiffy, and neither did my sleeping patterns. And it's the latter that landed me in trouble one day in class.

I'd always been the type of student who had a difficult time remaining attentive during class lectures, and my erratic sleep habits didn't help. One day in an Old Testament Bible class at Grand Canyon University, I dozed off to sleep. Unfortunately for me, of all the classes that I could have picked, I made the mistake of choosing the one with a unique class tradition. Toward the end of the class period, the professor called on a student to end the day's lecture with prayer.

Seeing the perfect opportunity to play a little joke, one of my buddies grabbed my shoulder and whispered that the instructor had just asked me to pray. In a state of complete disorientation, I looked up at the professor, noted his silence, and therefore naturally assumed that the class was waiting for me. So I stood up and began to pray.

"Dear Lord," I shouted out, "thank you for today's lecture. . . ." When the entire class broke out in laughter, I quickly realized that I had made a complete fool of myself. My gracious professor thanked me for the kind words, then asked me to wait until the end of class.

I remained extremely attentive for the remainder of the hour.

Please, learn from my embarrassment. Consider this sad little tale yet another reminder to remain attentive to your own self-care.

CHAPTER 9

Dance Step #5:

FINDING TREASURES IN TRIALS

Their voices rose in a great chorus of complaint against Moses and Aaron. "We wish we had died in Egypt, or even here in the wilderness!" they wailed. "Why is the Lord taking us to this country only to have us die in battle? Our wives and little ones will be carried off as slaves! Let's get out of here and return to Egypt!" Then they plotted among themselves, "Let's choose a leader and go back to Egypt!"

NUMBERS 14:2-4

PLEASE DON'T mistake me for Norman Vincent Peale, but I agree with the late author that we need to train ourselves to think positively. We cannot afford to bypass this critical skill; it's another crucial dance step in our marital repertoire. When problems beset a marriage, negative beliefs usually multiply and cause tremendous damage.

Back in 1977 Peale wrote a little article called "Worth Fighting For," in which he quoted his psychiatrist friend Smiley Blanton. Blanton wrote,

> To those who feel, as most of us do now and then, that marriage is not all it might be, I would recommend this: that somehow they find the time and the spirit to walk hand in hand with their marriage partner down some quiet street or

country road and contemplate the marvel and the mystery and the unimaginable beauty of the fact that there are two sexes, two diverse yet complementary kinds of human beings made for each other and for the stupendous purpose of the creation of life itself.

If you can bring yourself to consider . . . the power, the purpose, the magnificence of design that have gone into the creation of man and woman, then the petty daily differences and frictions will seem small and unworthy, and the wonder and privilege of being man and wife, of being married in heart, in mind, and in body, will shine forth again with the splendor that it had in the beginnings of romantic love—and with the glory that it still deserves to have.[1]

The right kind of positive thinking really can work wonders. And negative thinking can accomplish just as much—although in the other direction.

DEATH IN THE DESERT

God chose the wilderness as the classroom in which to teach his people the life skills they'd need in the Promised Land, but we shouldn't forget that the Hebrew nation spent a whole lot more time in the desert than it needed to. The Israelites spent forty years wandering among the sand dunes with the scorpions, and with the exception of Joshua and Caleb, not one person who left Egypt ever made it alive into the Promised Land.

Why not? The apostle Paul explains, "God was not pleased with most of them" (1 Corinthians 10:5). And why was God displeased? When you read the list of sins that Paul outlines in that passage, you note that several grow straight out of negative thinking. The last sin he mentions explicitly makes the connection: "Don't grumble as some of them did, for that is why God sent his angel of death to destroy them" (1 Corinthians 10:10).

Negative thinking, whether in the ancient Middle East or in your own marriage, can keep you in the wilderness for a long,

long time. Indulge negative thinking long enough, and eventually you'll experience your own death in the desert.

A POWERFUL FORCE FOR INTERPRETATION

Call negative thinking what you will—false or irrational beliefs, unrealistic expectations, self-defeating attitudes, unjustified negative explanations, or illogical conclusions—it powerfully affects how a spouse perceives and interprets what the other does. Research has shown that negative beliefs constitute one of the main reasons why couples divorce.[2]

We succumb to negative thinking when we consistently believe that the other person's motives are more negative than they really are, when we interpret our spouse's behavior to be much more negative than he or she intended. It comes down to this: Negative thinking believes that our spouse is trying to ruin or weaken our marriage *on purpose*. Listen to these examples:

- "You're always including your family. They've been between us our whole married life!"
- "You don't see it, do you? You're too negative, and it's driving me away!"
- "You say you're sorry, but you keep on doing the same mean things over and over. You'll never change!"

If the marriage runs into trouble, the repeated disappointments, arguments, and frustrations lead to a change in perspective. At that point we have a tendency to switch "lenses" and see our spouse differently—and almost entirely in a negative light.

Earlier we discussed confirmation bias and how it often sends couples into marital slavery. Whatever we believe about other people is what we tend to *see and hear*,

> **PROMISED LAND TIP**
> Whatever you believe about another person, positive or negative, you will find evidence of that belief in everything he or she says or does.

POSITIVE OR NEGATIVE?
YOU DECIDE

Your perception of your spouse is based on what you *see and hear*.

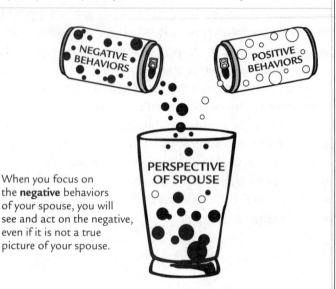

When you focus on the **negative** behaviors of your spouse, you will see and act on the negative, even if it is not a true picture of your spouse.

When you focus on the **positive** behaviors of your spouse, you will see and act on the positive.

even if it isn't true. If we believe someone is mean-spirited, then we see and hear everything through that grid.

If the glass in the graphic represents our heart and perspectives, then the diagram illustrates how we often put our negative perceptions into the glass, ignoring a spouse's good qualities. We put into our hearts the perception we have of our spouse's negative behavior. As a result, we continue to see and act on the negative, even if it does not paint a true picture of our spouse.

I think of the apostle Paul, who wrote in Romans, "If anyone regards something as unclean, then for him it is unclean" (14:14, NIV). And I remember the verse in Proverbs, "As he thinks in his heart, so is he" (23:7, NKJV).

People tend to live up or down to our beliefs about them. Therefore our expectations influence how we act toward our spouse, which in turn causes him or her to behave in a way consistent with our expectations. And our expectations become self-fulfilling prophecies.

One day I came home from work and found Erin in a bad mood. Something had clearly upset her. I instantly concluded that she was mad at me. I didn't ask her if this was true. I merely jumped to this conclusion. We were supposed to go on a date, and while we were driving, Erin didn't talk to me. Again, I interpreted her behavior as anger toward me. Finally I got so frustrated at her attitude (I couldn't think of a single reason why she should be angry with me) that I said, "I am so tired of your getting mad at me for no reason." I then expressed several more inflammatory statements. When I had finished accusing her, how do you think she responded? She got mad at me.

"What on earth are you talking about?" she demanded. "Why are you yelling at me?" We argued back and forth for another five minutes. Then we both withdrew. After several minutes of silence, Erin turned to me and said, "Just for your information, I was not mad at you. I got into a disagreement with a neighbor. This person had really hurt my feelings and I still felt upset when you got home. My bad mood had *nothing* to do with you."

My negative belief about Erin (that she was angry with me

for no reason) became a self-fulfilling prophecy. My behavior prompted her to become mad at me. Thus my original faulty interpretation became a reality.

In the late 1960s, Jane Elliott, a third-grade teacher in Riceville, Iowa, grew concerned that her young students had no real idea of racism or prejudice. The children, all white and Christian, lived in rural Iowa. One day, Elliott divided her class by eye color. She told her students that blue-eyed people were better than brown-eyed people—smarter, nicer, more trustworthy, and so on. The brown-eyed kids had to wear cloth collars around their necks so that they could be instantly recognizable as part of the inferior group. The blue-eyed kids got to play longer at recess, could have second helpings at the cafeteria, received abundant praise in the classroom, and so on.

How did the children respond? In less than half an hour, Elliott created a prejudiced society. While the children had cooperated as a cohesive group before the experiment, they suddenly became divided. The "superior" kids, the blue-eyed ones, made fun of the brown-eyed kids, refused to play with them, tattled on them to the teacher, thought up new restrictions and punishments for them, and even started a fistfight with them in the school yard. The "inferior" kids, the brown-eyed ones, felt depressed and demoralized. They did significantly poorer on classroom tests. In fact, they became shadows of their formerly happy selves.

The next day, Elliott switched the stereotypes about eye color. She said she had made a mistake—that brown-eyed people were really the superior ones. She told the brown-eyed kids to put their collars on the blue-eyed kids. They gleefully did so. The tables had turned—and the brown-eyed kids exacted their revenge.

Jane Elliott's now-famous experiment demonstrated in a powerful way that when negative thinking consistently invades a relationship, it produces an environment of hopelessness and demoralization.[3] Negatively perceived people lack any motivation to change their behavior because no matter what they do, it will get framed in a negative light.

Pastor and author Charles Swindoll once said:

> The longer I live, the more I realize the impact of attitude on life. Attitude, to me, is more important than facts. It is more important than the past, than education, than money, than circumstances, than failures, than successes, than what other people think or say or do. It is more important than appearance, giftedness, or skill. It will make or break a company . . . a church . . . a home. The remarkable thing is we have a choice every day regarding the attitude we will embrace for that day. We cannot change our past; we cannot change the fact that people will act in a certain way. We cannot change the inevitable. The one thing that we can do is play on the one string we have, and that is our attitude. I am convinced that life is 10% what happens to me and 90% how I react to it. And so it is with you. We are in charge of our attitudes.[4]

In a toxic marital environment, it's often not the words or deeds themselves that cause trouble, but the meaning that a spouse attaches to them. Very often the "offending" spouse has done nothing to convey or create that meaning. But once people attach a meaning to an event, they likely will accept their interpretation without feeling any need for confirmation. And so the relationship continues to deteriorate.

FOUR STEPS TO COMBAT NEGATIVE THINKING

So how do we fight negative thinking? I do not advocate some kind of Pollyanna mentality. We cannot sit around wishing or hoping that our spouse will change truly negative behaviors.

But we do need to consider that our partner's motives are more positive than we have previously imagined. We must learn to replace negative thoughts with positive ones. On a very practical level, that means to methodically focus on what a spouse does *right*. Let me suggest four practical steps toward battling negative thinking.

Step 1: Ask Yourself, "Could I Be Wrong?"

Could it be that you have interpreted your spouse's actions in an overly negative way? Perhaps some of your misunderstandings stem from differences in perspectives, not from some negative trait in your spouse.

One day while driving home from the office, I called Erin. As soon as she answered the phone, I knew something was wrong. I even asked, "Hon, is something wrong?" And then she used the four words I most hate to hear: "We need to talk." Anytime I hear these words from Erin, combined with an upset tone of voice, it usually means that I am in trouble. As soon as she said it, my heart sank. I rolled my eyes and immediately started to think of how I could defend myself. I even said, "Whatever!"

The funny part? I didn't have a clue what she wanted to talk about. Regardless, I jumped to the conclusion that I was in big trouble. In hindsight, I should have told myself, "Although this statement usually means I'm in trouble, I could be wrong."

Step 2: Substitute a More Reasonable Response for the Negative Thought

When I heard, "We need to talk," I immediately felt anxious, and my brain flooded with negative thoughts. At that moment I could have substituted a more reasonable response: "Maybe she wants to talk about something positive that I've done. And even if Erin is upset, it will last only a short time. Even if I did something to upset her, I do plenty of positive things as well." Any one of these thoughts could have kept me from jumping to conclusions and allowing negative beliefs to build up about my wife.

Step 3: Check Out the Accuracy of Your Negative Thinking

Consider alternative explanations for what your spouse does. Look for supporting evidence, contradictory evidence, alternative explanations, and more logical conclusions. Push yourself to look for evidence contrary to the negative interpretation you usually take. You can accomplish this either by directly asking your spouse or by making further observations of your partner's actions.

When I walked into the house and found Erin sitting at the table, it took every ounce of emotional strength I had to walk over and give her a kiss on the cheek. I also wanted to see if she'd let me kiss her. If so, that would be a good sign that, just maybe, I wasn't in big trouble. She did let me kiss her. So far, so good!

"Erin," I said as I sat down, "by the way you talked to me on the phone, I have to admit I feel like I'm in trouble. What have I done wrong?"

"What are you talking about?" Erin said, almost laughing. "You didn't do anything. I had a bad experience with a friend, and I really need your advice about how I should handle it."

"I was just kidding," I joked, a jittery laugh escaping my throat. Not only was I not in trouble, she actually wanted me to help her solve a problem! What an irony!

Time and time again, these first three steps have helped me combat negative beliefs. The moment something happens to which I have a negative reaction, I try to quickly think: *I could be wrong. Although I'm 99 percent positive I know exactly what she meant by that, I might have misread her motives.* Substituting a more reasonable thought can provide me with other alternatives for the person's actions or words that have hurt me: *Maybe she misunderstood something I said. Maybe she's had a bad day. Maybe she has some negative beliefs about me.*

Whatever alternative thought you substitute, it can really help stop the cascading negative beliefs and conclusions. But you have to check out your more positive alternative scenario. It won't work simply to substitute a more reasonable thought and then leave it alone. The fact is, you do *not* know. Your original, negative thought could be right. So if you don't check it out, you miss the opportunity to understand the other person. You might miss the chance to seek forgiveness. If you don't check it out, you let the other person off the hook and you end up trying to work out the issue by yourself. This never benefits the relationship.

Remember Dr. John Gottman's "cascade of isolation" mentioned earlier? In one step of this negative cycle, we start working out our problems without involving the other person. Keep this destructive pattern from invading your relationship by always checking out your negative beliefs or conclusions.

Step 4: Keep Track of Positive Behavior

Couples must learn to note the positive things their spouses do and then respond accordingly. For a start, try to methodically notice your spouse's positive behavior. By noticing actions that please you, you will begin to really look at your spouse. This will force you to break through the barriers that obstruct your vision of your partner's good deeds.

Psychologist Dr. Mark Goldstein once gave a group of couples on the brink of divorce a single assignment. "Go home and write all of the positive things that your partner does throughout the week. Write nothing else. Do it as a competition. I'll reward the winner."

> **PROMISED LAND TIP**
> Focusing on your spouse's positive behavior is the key to fighting negative beliefs.

The result was that 70 percent of the couples who went on this treasure hunt reported a significant improvement in their level of marriage satisfaction. They thanked Dr. Goldstein and praised his efforts—but he rightfully explained that they had done the work.[5] Their marriages began to improve when they started to change their perception of their spouse and began focusing on the positive. Once they felt better about their relationship, they started to act differently within their relationship. The exercise had a snowball effect.

Focusing on the positives can help you foster positive beliefs about your spouse for the long term. When Erin said that we needed to talk and I jumped to a negative conclusion, something gave me the ability to give her the benefit of the doubt and to substitute more reasonable thoughts. I focused on positive things about her, not just the negative. I had built up a nice surplus of positive beliefs about Erin because I have disciplined myself to notice many of the positive things she does.

CHOOSING HAPPINESS

Happiness is largely a choice. By thinking rightly and positively, we can begin to change a bad situation into a good one.

I love the apostle Paul's take on this idea: "Fix your thoughts on what is true and honorable and right. Think about things that are pure and lovely and admirable. Think about things that are excellent and worthy of praise" (Philippians 4:8).

Whenever someone asks me for an autograph, I write the reference "Philippians 4:8" next to my name. That verse offers one of my favorite pieces of marriage advice, and it has nothing explicitly to do with marriage. When we focus on the positive, when we let our minds dwell on the true and the honorable, the right and the pure, the lovely and the admirable—when we concentrate on things excellent and praiseworthy—we set ourselves up for success, in marriage and elsewhere.

This is not a Pollyanna fantasy, as some have scoffed. The practice is thoroughly biblical, and it powerfully shapes the way you and I relate to others, including our spouses.

A woman came to see a divorce lawyer, determined to dump her husband. She hated her spouse and told the attorney she wanted to hurt him as much as possible.

"I can help you with that," the lawyer said. "Here's what you do. Go home and be incredibly nice to your husband for three months. Compliment him on his appearance, on his intelligence, on his ability to run a home. Make him feel as though you're still head over heels in love with him. Then when he least expects it, serve him with divorce papers. You'll cut his heart out."

The woman loved the diabolical idea and went home to put it into practice. When the divorce lawyer didn't hear from his prospective client for more than four months, he called her to see how their plan was working. "Are you ready to divorce him now?" the attorney asked.

"*Divorce* him?" the woman asked incredulously. "Why on earth would I want to divorce him? I'm married to the most wonderful man in the whole world!"

Don't underestimate the power of positive thinking. A more effective dance step is hard to find. Find the positive in each situation, and look at the blessings and gifts God has given you. Look for the good or positive aspects of your spouse's behavior. Look for the silver lining in the dark rain clouds. Learn to see the glass as half-full, not half-empty. You can handle every situation that confronts you either positively or negatively.

Choose the positive! And then see the great results in your marriage. You just might find yourself waking up inside a dream.

TAKING IT A STEP FURTHER

It's great to give a spouse the benefit of the doubt and to wrack our brains for a more positive explanation for some puzzling or difficult behavior that confronts us. But I think it's wise to take this positive approach a little further. I think it makes sense to go on regular treasure hunting expeditions for the positive things our spouses do. We all benefit when we find treasures in our trials.

I wish I could point to several examples of ancient Israel's doing its own treasure hunting in the wilderness, but I can't. The generation that died in the desert never could kick its habit of faultfinding and negative thinking.

Do you know how many times the word *rejoiced* appears in the narrative of Israel's time in the wilderness? Zero. Can you guess how often the word *happy* is used? Never. How about the word *glad*? Not once. The word *joy* appears just one time, in Leviticus 9:24, when the priests began their ministry at the beginning of the nation's desert experience. When fire came out from the presence of the Lord and consumed some burnt offerings, all the people saw it and shouted for joy.

Apparently it was the last time they whooped it up in the wilderness.

Now, could they have found things to celebrate in the middle of their trials? No doubt. Whenever they found water even in a harsh and arid place, they could have rejoiced. But they didn't. When God spoke to Moses to let the people know where to go next, they could have given thanks. They refused. When God foiled the plans of their enemies or when he miraculously prevented their shoes and clothes from wearing out or when he spared the life of an Israelite bitten by a poisonous snake, the people could have felt glad and expressed their joy. Instead they kept silent, except to complain and grumble and murmur and grouse.

They never learned how to hunt for treasure. And they never found any.

FROM BITTER TO BETTER

Couples who have grown bitter and resentful need to understand that the essence of treasure hunting is the ability to transform *bitter* into *better*. Those who feel bitter suffer from anger and low self-worth. Those who feel better become grateful and enjoy an elevated sense of value. One way to help increase your self-worth and decrease anger is to teach yourself to find "lemonade" within your own "lemon-filled" circumstances.

Here's an exercise for you. Create a chart that will help you recognize the positive results of the difficult things that happen in your marriage. Take a clean sheet of paper, and divide it into two columns. Each element will have its own column. Use as many sheets of paper as necessary, the more the better.

1. *Write down the most painful trials you've endured in your marriage.* In the first column, list the main trials in your marriage that have caused you pain, especially the ones that have lowered your self-esteem or where you felt shame or guilt. It may be too painful to list them all, but do just that, if you are able. If it be-

comes unbearable, focus on two or three and deal with the others some other time.

Listing your trials can be very helpful in identifying the treasures you've gained. Sometimes, however, reliving those hurtful times can uncover major pain that you've buried.

2. *List all the benefits for each trial.* The second column represents the very heart and life of your own treasures. You not only wear these treasures but also display them on your favorite trophy shelf.

Start listing the positive aspects of each of the painful encounters in your marriage. Crisis situations tend to make us more loving and compassionate. They also heighten other benefits, including things such as:

Thoughtfulness	Perseverance
Gentleness	Sensitivity
Carefulness	Endurance
Kindness	Humility
Patience	Maturity
Greater self-control	Drawing the family closer
Strength	together
Courage	Increased awareness of
Genuine love	others' needs and pain
Righteousness	

It might be valuable for you to ask the people who know and love you to describe any benefits they see from your having gone through trials. They can often add a perspective that you may have overlooked.

God promises that he will make us complete through trials. "Consider it pure joy . . . whenever you face trials of many kinds, because you know that the testing of your faith develops perseverance. Perseverance must finish its work so that you may be mature and complete, not lacking anything" (James 1:2-4, NIV). How have you become more mature through your trials?

Note that the attributes of love listed in 1 Corinthians 13 resemble the types of treasures that many people gain as a result of trials: "Love is patient and kind. Love is not jealous or boastful or proud or rude. Love does not demand its own way. Love is not irritable, and it keeps no record of when it has been wronged. It is never glad about injustice but rejoices whenever the truth wins out. Love never gives up, never loses faith, is always hopeful, and endures through every circumstance. . . . There are three things that will endure—faith, hope, and love—and the greatest of these is love" (1 Corinthians 13:4-7, 13). Going through a trial almost always results in increasing our sensitivity, which is the basis of love. We become more sensitive when we get beat up. Our compassion grows when we know how suffering people feel, and we become more caring, thoughtful, and gentle. All of these things come out of pain.

Difficult experiences also cause us to slow down and realize that people are more important than anything else. Have you ever talked with people who have suffered a heart attack or have endured cancer treatment? These people are never the same. Everything changes. Heart attacks and cancer also help their victims to become more loving. They more readily feel the pain of others. They develop an intuitive sense of what others need because they've already been through it.

> **PROMISED LAND TIP**
> God promises to give us treasures as we go through trials. That's his guarantee! Our job is to find the treasure buried in our hearts.

FINDING TREASURE IN UNLIKELY PLACES

Remember, it's always possible to find treasure in the worst of circumstances. I've seen this principle in action in my own family as well as in the lives of countless others.

It had become a regular occurrence. Jill's husband stayed late at the office and attended out-of-town business meetings without her. Finally the truth emerged that he was having an affair. After many angry confrontations, he decided to move out. Listen to how she describes what happened next:

That day is still fresh in my mind. "I'm moving out today!" my husband Mark announced in a cold, distant voice. "They're delivering a bed to my apartment in a few hours. I'll be back later to pick up my clothes and other personal belongings." And with that, my husband was gone.

I stood there, looking bewildered. There were so many things I wanted to say to make him stay. There were so many things that I wanted to say to make him pay. After all, he was the one that had the affair. But most of all, I just wanted my marriage to work out.

With that in mind, the only thing I could manage to say was, "Fine." I had to go to work that day knowing that when I came home, my husband would no longer be living there.

The rest of our separation is not so clearly etched in my mind like the day Mark left. For a while he lived alone in the city. But during this time he would call me, show up, or we would have "dates." We would try to reconcile. We would get along really well, but then I would find out he was still seeing this other woman. Then we'd have a huge fight, and he'd be back to his place in the city. I would be left wondering if this was the final straw that would break the back of our marriage.

We cycled through this dance for about a year. Yet, I believe several positive things happened during that year—especially for me as a person. For example, I got a new job and spent time cultivating several deep friendships. These things helped establish my own identity as an individual. I was beginning to feel stronger and better able to be alone. But then Mark would show up or would set up a time for us to be together. We would fall right back in step with our relational dance. We would argue because I knew that he had just been with her. So I was consistently angry and irritable because I felt as if I was being repeatedly betrayed. This was our dance.

Looking back on that time, I can see that I did many things to compromise my own self. I sent a lot of cards, I called him a lot on the phone, and I tried to be the perfect cook when we were together. To be more physically attractive, I lost weight and frequented the local tanning salon. I can remember thinking, *Well, this may be good for him, but it's definitely not good for me.* But I came to the conclusion that something first had to be good for me—my self-image and self-esteem—before it could be good for us relationally. If I was miserable, then I would never be able to build a satisfying relationship with my husband.

Ultimately, I learned that weight loss and exercise should be done for my health and not just for my appearance or to win back my man. I also realized that I needed to develop my own interests and to learn how to take care of myself financially. Thus, I gained self-esteem knowing that I could work and support myself.

The bottom line was that I became so tired of trying to please Mark by being the "perfect" wife—like the ones in the movies and magazines. I finally started leaving him alone. Over time, we started to communicate some. We even began to learn about our most basic relational needs. I feel that this marked the turning point in our relationship.

As Jill began taking care of herself and becoming the whole person God had created her to be, she began looking for (and finding!) positive qualities in herself and in her marriage. With that change in attitude, her relationship with her husband began to improve. After a season of dating and focusing on the positives, here's what happened:

Mark moved back into our home after almost one year of counseling and learning new relationship skills. We are still on the journey toward having a satisfying marriage. In winning back my husband, the greatest thing I've learned is the importance of understanding my own needs and the needs of others, not just my husband's needs. As I learned to take care of myself, it has been a major factor in bridging the gap in our marital distance.

I could go on and on with stories from our lives and from the many letters I've received from couples who have found great treasures in their trials. I'm confident, however, that by hunting for treasures, you also can find hope in times of turmoil. The following poem, whose author is unknown, beautifully illustrates the essence of treasure hunting:

> My life is but a weaving, between my God and me,
>   I do not choose the colors, He worketh steadily.
> Oftimes He weaveth sorrow, and I in foolish pride,
>   Forget He sees the upper, and I the underside.
>
> Not till the loom is silent, and shuttles cease to fly,
>   Will God unroll the canvas and explain the
>   reason why.
> The dark threads are as needful in the skillful Weaver's
>   hand,
>   As the threads of gold and silver in the pattern He has
>   planned.

DOORWAY TO INTIMACY

The dance steps I've outlined can all be rapidly applied, and not only in distressed relationships. Healthy marriages can grow even healthier through increasing application of honor, self-care, and finding treasures in the trials. But don't imagine that healthy couples who learn and practice these dance steps avoid all conflict! These skills are designed not to eliminate conflict but to enable couples to work through conflict in a healthy way.

Conflict, as my dad has long taught, is actually a doorway to intimacy. Some couples have battled for so long that they become hypersensitive toward conflict. They become paranoid of it, like a frightened deer spooked by every sound in the woods. Conflict so unnerves them that they avoid it at all costs—and so make a costly error.

Conflict is not something to be avoided but something to be navigated. If we want to get to the deeper levels of a relationship, we have to go *through* conflict. By entering the door of conflict, we learn more about each other and our relationship. In every kind of conflict, a golden nugget waits to be unearthed, as the next chapter will reveal. And why would anyone shy away from such rare treasure?

CHAPTER 10

Dance Step #6:

RESOLVING CONFLICT THROUGH COMMUNICATION

Moses' father-in-law replied, "What you are doing is not good. You and these people who come to you will only wear yourselves out. The work is too heavy for you; you cannot handle it alone. Listen now to me and I will give you some advice, and may God be with you."

EXODUS 18:17-19, NIV

FOR THE FIRST four years of our marriage, Erin and I struggled painfully with a money issue that surfaced just after our honeymoon. It gained so much momentum that we couldn't even talk about it. While I can look back now and easily identify the problem, I couldn't back then. We could never understand its power over us.

Before our honeymoon, I had saved up one thousand dollars for us to spend however we desired. Each of us got five hundred dollars. I thought it was neat; she thought it was awesome.

Although we had never talked about it, I expected that we could do whatever we wanted with that money. Erin could give it away, buy five hundred dollars' worth of toothpicks or a trunk full of lemon drops; I couldn't have cared less. It was her money, and she could do with it as she pleased. In the same way, I thought I could spend my half of the money however I wanted to.

Such an arrangement probably would have worked fine had we talked about it beforehand. But we didn't. I had no idea that Erin and I held completely different expectations about how to use that money.

Erin generally doesn't like us to handle our money individually. She loves to feel connected through our finances and wants to talk ahead of time about our purchases. Remember, her fear is not feeling validated. She wants to feel that I value her thoughts and feelings. And one of the best ways to validate her is by talking and sharing.

While I knew this, I misunderstood her need; it felt very controlling to me. I thought she wanted to approve how I wanted to spend my money, and that didn't sit well with me. Remember, I want to feel successful, and talking about my purchases threatened my sense of success. She often has her own opinions on how to spend money, and when our opinions don't agree, I feel like a failure.

The situation didn't turn into a big deal . . . until after the honeymoon.

When we returned from Hawaii, we had about ten days before my graduate classes began. One day we jumped in my pickup truck, threw in all our camping gear, and drove north from Denver to Montana. Somewhere along the line, we ran into a little town. While Erin went off to explore for a bit on her own, I saw an antique store. We both love antiques. With a wad of remaining money in my pocket, I went into the store and saw the coolest collection of old sporting paraphernalia. I found an old leather football helmet, priced at $250, and I knew it was worth much more than that. I slapped my money down so fast that I practically broke the counter.

When I reconnected with my bride a little later and excitedly told her about my purchase, she responded as if I had stolen her nest egg. A huge argument erupted, and it quickly turned into a very painful conflict. Immediately we slid into a destructive dance, although we weren't aware of the dance at the time. She questioned why I had bought the helmet, which made me feel as if I had somehow failed. So I tried to cope by seizing control. "Listen," I said, "this isn't an area that we even need to discuss." Of course, she felt invalidated, and the whole dreary cycle began to pick up steam. We got stuck and couldn't extricate ourselves.

Over the next four years the money issue took on tremendous momentum. Erin got angry with me whenever I bought anything without first talking to her. It became a total mess—ridiculous, now that we look back on it—but at the time it caused us a tremendous amount of pain.

Then one day I had to travel from Los Angeles to San Diego to attend a conference called PREP, led by Dr. Scott Stanley and Dr. Howard Markman.[1] Erin came with me. There we learned a communication skill called the *speaker-listener method*. It revolutionized our marriage. Today the team at the Smalley Marriage Institute calls our version of this method *LUV Talk*, and I'm convinced that it can do for your relationship what it did for ours.

LUV TALK IS NOT ROCKET SCIENCE

LUV is an acronym for **L**isten, **U**nderstand, and **V**alidate. We find the fundamental truth underpinning LUV Talk in the New Testament, which counsels us, "My dear brothers and sisters, be quick to listen, slow to speak, and slow to get angry" (James 1:19). This phenomenal verse provides the road map to healthy communication and reveals the essence of LUV Talk.

LUV Talk is not rocket science. Every reputable counselor teaches some form of it. LUV Talk gives us a method to talk through difficult issues. If we are to walk through the doorway of conflict in order to reach a deep level of intimacy, we need to learn the dance step of effective communication.

Before I plunge into specifics, let me give you a promise: If you can learn to apply LUV Talk in your marriage, you will be able to reach win-win solutions in all of your conflicts. And don't fool yourself! The only real choice a couple has in resolving conflict is win-win. Win-lose is impossible because if one partner feels like a loser, then both partners have lost.

The Bible tells us that in marriage, the "two are united into one."[2] When we unite as husband and wife, we form a team. Is it possible during a baseball game for some teammates to win a game while other teammates lose? Hardly. When one team member loses, the whole team loses. The same is true in marriage. When you play on the same team, both of you win or both of you lose; there is no middle ground. LUV Talk can help you to win.

THANK YOU, McDONALD'S

When couples launch fully into their dance, they find it impossible to talk to each other productively. Their dance prevents them from talking through differences of opinion, disagreements, or other conflicts. And even after they break the power of their dance, they still need a new dance step with the power to help them resolve their conflicts successfully. Enter LUV Talk.

Anytime you get embroiled in a serious conflict or uncover a major difference of opinion, LUV Talk helps you to set your own opinions or issues on the shelf in order to enter into a specific kind of healing dialogue. Your conversation looks very much like what occurs every day at a McDonald's drive-through.

As you pull up to the speaker, you read the menu and give your order. And then what happens? Someone says back to you what you just ordered. You listen carefully to make sure the person got it right. If the person got your order wrong, you say, "That was close, but I didn't want a Coke, I wanted a diet Coke," or "I wanted a large order of fries, not a small order." You go back and forth with the disembodied voice until the order taker can accurately say back to you what you want. Then you pull forward, pay, receive your order, and check it one last time to make sure it's right. When all seems in order, you drive off.

Did you know that McDonald's spent millions of dollars in customer research to develop its drive-through system? Many years ago the restaurant chain found that customers were not returning because they felt frustrated with their drive-through experience. When the company studied the problem, it found a solution connected to the way its employees responded to orders. It discovered that the order taker had to accurately repeat what the customer wanted, without any kind of additional commentary. Management learned that employees often offered unsolicited commentary, such as, "What about a sundae with that?" and the extra feedback distorted the communication.

Imagine that a pimply-faced employee responded to my order of a Big Mac and a large order of fries with a curt, "I can see you in the car, and do you realize that we now offer salads? Because that stuff you ordered has a lot of fat."

How would I feel? I would feel enraged, pull forward, and demand to speak to Ronald McDonald himself. Or more likely, I'd never return. I'd divorce McDonald's.

Since the restaurant desperately wants to avoid even a trial separation, it developed some new rules for how the conversation ought to flow in order to satisfy the customer. It may surprise you that those rules apply amazingly well to couples who want to turn their conflict into pathways of understanding and healing.

In brief, here's how LUV Talk works: When conflict arises, one spouse becomes the "customer" and the other the "employee." This distinction is crucial because the customer and the employee each has his or her own set of rules to follow. We often encourage couples to use some sort of object to identify who is taking which role; whoever holds the object is designated the customer. Naturally, some objects are more appropriate than others! Sharp objects, lethal weapons, or elements of mass destruction do not make for good discussions. Stay with soft, cuddly items, just in case conflict erupts.

All of us want to feel understood, especially during a conflict. Keep that in mind when using LUV Talk because if you start blaming, accusing, or becoming frustrated—your old coping strategies—your responses will only prevent you from receiving what you truly desire, which is understanding and validation.

Rules for the Customer

The customer has only three major rules to follow. These rules keep the person focused and the conflict structured to ensure complete understanding.

RULE 1: SPEAK WITH "I" STATEMENTS

The most important rule for the customer is to speak with "I" statements. Too often a couple in conflict starts playing the blame game. *You* this and *you* that permeate the conversation to the point where the employee or listener can no longer do a good job because he or she is concentrating on defending against the accusations.

I can always come up with at least two ways of saying the same thing. I could say, "Why can't you get your act together and clean up your mess!" or I could say, "When I come home to a messy house, I get frustrated." Can you see the difference in tone? The first example sounds aggressive and demeaning, and it attacks the character of the listener. The second example sticks with how the situation made the customer feel; suddenly the statement seems softer and allows the listener to hear and receive the statement.

RULE 2: DESCRIBE ONLY FEELINGS AND NEEDS

Describe only feelings and needs when using "I" statements. Say, "I feel . . ." or "I need . . ." This is a key aspect of LUV Talk. This rule keeps the conflict from escalating out of control and allows the customer to get a true understanding of his or her feelings and needs.

In my dad's book *Secrets to Lasting Love,* he describes five levels of intimacy, moving from shallow (the first level) to deep (the fifth level).[3] Levels four and five require couples to discuss their feelings and needs in safety. Most couples begin marriage by safely discussing their feelings and needs. But if one or both invalidate or belittle the other, the safety and intimacy levels decrease.

Sticking strictly to feelings and needs also keeps us from blaming, which only inflames marital conflicts. An employee is far more likely to hear, "When the trash isn't taken out, I feel frustrated, and I need a system to be in place to ensure that the trash is taken out every week" than to hear, "This place is a pigsty. You can't keep anything clean."

If you are the customer, your goal ought to be to give your spouse a gift: a clear understanding of who you are. But the key is to understand the *emotion*. When I'm in the customer role, my gift to my wife is to truly understand myself so that I can tell her what I think and feel, but especially how I feel. As the employee, her gift in return is to listen to my emotions and feelings and to help me feel understood and validated. Her gift is to really "get" who I am and how I feel. If she is to understand who I am, I need to understand myself and be able to express that understanding to her. I need to be able to say, "I felt ____, and this is what I would have liked to see happen." The reverse is true when she's the customer. Then my job as the employee is to understand her and her emotions and feelings—and I can do that well only to the extent that she understands herself and can express that understanding to me. We take turns playing both roles. That's how this process avoids becoming self-centered.

It is so important to understand emotions and feelings. I often have a hard time coming up with precise feeling words, even though I'm a professional counselor. With that in mind, I'd like to offer the following chart. In the past I actually posted this "cheat sheet" on our kitchen refrigerator and literally grabbed it to help me convey more accurately how I felt. Often I just couldn't identify all the ways I felt; I just knew I was feeling *something*. The following list really helped me. Maybe it will help you, too.

MILD	MODERATE	STRONG	INTENSE
Unpopular	Suspicious	Disgusted	Hated
Jealous	Envious	Resentful	Unloved
Listless	Dejected	Frustrated	Angry
Moody	Unhappy	Sad	Hurt
Lethargic	Bored	Depressed	Miserable
Gloomy	Bad	Sick	Painful
Discontented	Disappointed	Dissatisfied	Cynical
Tired	Wearied	Fatigued	Exhausted
Indifferent	Torn up	Worn out	Worthless
Unsure	Inadequate	Useless	Impotent
Impatient	Irritated	Weak	Futile
Dependent	Helpless	Hopeless	Abandoned
Unimportant	Resigned	Forlorn	Estranged
Regretful	Apathetic	Rejected	Degraded
Sheepish	Embarrassed	Shamed	Guilty
Bashful	Shy	Embarrassed	Humiliated
Self-conscious	Uncomfortable	Inhibited	Alienated
Puzzled	Baffled	Bewildered	Shocked
Edgy	Confused	Frightened	Panicky
Upset	Nervous	Anxious	Trapped
Reluctant	Tempted	Dismayed	Horrified
Timid	Tense	Apprehensive	Afraid
Mixed-up	Worried	Dreadful	Scared
Baffled	Perplexed	Disturbed	Terrified
Sullen	Disdainful	Antagonistic	Infuriated

When you can differentiate and express how you're truly feeling, it allows your spouse to truly "get" you. And that's wonderful!

RULE 3: KEEP STATEMENTS SHORT AND CONCISE
It is vital that customers keep their statements short and concise since employees have to repeat what the customer says. Cus-

tomers who give thirty-minute statements of feelings and needs overwhelm the employee and make it impossible for him or her to understand, let alone process, the order.

The average couple in conflict typically floods the situation with many words. But too many words to describe feelings and needs make it difficult to resolve conflict. Keep your statements to short, bite-size pieces.

If you as the customer can keep these three rules, you will greatly increase your chances of being understood.

Rules for the Employee

We find the heart of LUV Talk in the rules for the employee. As an employee, you must **Listen, Understand,** and **Validate** if you want to resolve your marital conflicts.

Did you know that the average couple spends more than *twenty years* arguing about the same thing?[4] It's true. Couples rarely get to the heart of the conflict because they seldom understand what they are really arguing about. If you want to resolve your future conflicts, you'd be wise to learn how to LUV.

RULE 1: LISTEN

We hear words every second of every day, but most of us don't truly *listen*. What's the difference? It's big. Maybe a change in terminology will help us to better understand.

Hearing and listening are two different things. Unless we're deaf, we naturally hear sound; but we listen only when we consciously attempt to pay attention to the needs and feelings of those around us—especially the feelings and emotions. We hear quite naturally, but we listen by choice.

Listening also requires more than our ears. We listen with our eyes, with our body language, and with our heart. When our spouse talks, we maintain eye contact, nod our head, and posture our body in our spouse's direction. All of these signs give our spouse the feeling we are truly listening and not just pretending.

The most fundamental aspect of listening is repeating what

our spouse says—especially the feelings and emotions. Remember, our spouse is the customer and is supposed to describe his or her feelings and needs in short statements. The employee's job is to repeat what the customer says. When the employee does that, the customer gets the chance to correct the order.

It's at this point that most conversations go bad.

As humans, we tend to misunderstand, misinterpret, or draw the wrong conclusions during the communication process. How easy it is to misunderstand and draw the wrong conclusion!

Before Erin and I got married, we lived near Phoenix, very close to Squaw Peak. We often hiked in and around Squaw Peak Park, but when local kids started drinking and having sex there, the city took steps to clean up the place. The police did a good job, and families started showing up again.

One day Erin and I went hiking in the park. Afterward we planned to eat dinner and then go to a movie. By about 5:30, we had hiked up to a spot no more than forty or fifty feet off the ground, to a ledge that hung out over the parking lot. From there we could keep our eyes on our vehicle while still getting an incredible view of Phoenix. Often we'd take some food up there and just sit and talk. On this day we brought some fruit juice.

While we enjoyed ourselves, a patrol car came by, and the police officer apparently thought we were consuming alcohol. He yelled up at us, "What are you guys doing?"

The distance muffled his words, and I asked Erin, "What did he say?"

"I think he wants to know what we're doing," she answered.

"Oh, I bet he thinks that we're drinking," I said. I suspected that from that distance, we looked pretty young; he probably mistook us for a couple of high schoolers.

So I yelled out, "Juice! It's okay!"

He didn't seem impressed. "Come on down!" he shouted. "What are you guys doing?"

I continued to try to communicate with him. I pointed at

my watch and yelled, "We're almost ready to leave. *Juice!*" We needed to leave at six, so I shouted, "We're leaving at six!"

"What?" he yelled back.

"Six!"

At that moment, many of the families present started to laugh. He did, too. We decided we ought to make our way down to clear up the confusion. When we met the policeman, we showed him the juice.

"What were you saying up there?" he asked.

"I said, 'We are leaving at six.' "

"Oh!" he replied. "I thought you were saying 'sex.' "

We had a good laugh about it; so did everyone else there that day. But what we did not have was good communication. Isn't it easy to draw the wrong conclusion when someone else is talking?

Understand that to have good communication you're more than a parrot or a robot. Don't repeat your spouse's statements word for word. Try instead to say back the emotional flavor of the statements. What was the emotional effect of what the other person experienced? That's the true nugget.

As I look back on my own marriage and as I look at every couple I've counseled, I see listening as an important key to marital success. If we can just learn how to listen, both as an art and as a skill, we will build satisfying relationships.

RULE 2: UNDERSTAND

We seek understanding by asking questions. If we feel confused by what our spouse has said or if we sense that something may be missing, we ask. In the heat of battle, of course, such a thing doesn't occur to us. But when we get fully engaged in LUV Talk, the very structure of the method allows us to calm down and think rationally. And when we think rationally, good questions often arise.

> **PROMISED LAND TIP**
> As you learn how to listen, both as an art and as a skill, you will be building the kind of relationships that are truly satisfying.

"I hear you saying that you get frustrated when I don't take out the trash," you might say. "But may I ask a question? I don't think I completely understand just how frustrated you are. Can you help me understand that?"

"It sounds like you were hurt last night when I didn't call to tell you that I'd be late. Tell me more about the hurt. Zero to ten, with ten being the most hurt, how much did that hurt you?"

"Am I hearing you right that you felt degraded when I made that comment at the party last night? Help me understand that better. What do you mean by 'degraded'?"

Questions can help in the journey toward understanding. They allow you to go deeper in your communication with your spouse. They allow you to unravel the mystery surrounding conflict. In short, questions allow us to gain answers. By asking questions, you try to understand how this person felt about himself or herself. However, be very careful with questions. Never use questions as a way to argue or disagree with what your spouse is saying. Questions should always be aimed at understanding the other person at a deeper level. A question should not be about you. You will get the opportunity to focus on you when you are the customer.

PROMISED LAND TIP
Use questions to gain a deeper understanding, but never use questions as a way to argue or disagree with the speaker.

At this stage, you're not trying to solve anything. The solution is completely separate. Listening and understanding are part of Plan A. Solutions are part of Plan B.

Suppose you went to the doctor and told him, "I've had this pain on the right side," and he instantly prescribed some medication or wanted to schedule you for surgery. Wouldn't you say, "Now, wait a minute! I was about to describe ten other symptoms I also have"? Or what if he started arguing with you: "Are you sure it's there and not here?"

We would never (or should never) allow a doctor to diagnose and treat a problem without first getting a complete picture of our symptoms. If we want an effective cure, we need to give our physician a full understanding of our problem.

The same thing is true in a relationship. We can't get to an effective solution without first acquiring a full understanding of the problem.

Many people often err at this point by focusing on the content of their spouse's statements. Suppose a spouse says, "I feel hurt when you come home late from work." The listener might say back, "So it's really difficult for you when I come home late from work."

Such a response misses the point. The employee has to focus on the customer's emotions and feelings. Your spouse's *feelings* should be your primary concern. Often this is hard to identify because the speaker won't offer any emotions: "It's just rough on me when you come home late from work." In that case, the listener can offer, tentatively, "I hear you say it's rough. But are you saying it's actually really hurtful or frustrating?"

"Yes, it's very frustrating."

"So it sounds as if it may be even beyond frustrating; maybe it's even painful."

"Yes!"

When you listen for feelings and emotions, LUV Talk *works*.

RULE 3: VALIDATE

Now we come to the core of the employee's job description. Validation is allowing your spouse to be an individual, to express feelings and needs that may differ from your own.

You invalidate our spouse whenever you put your own thoughts and feelings into him or her and don't allow your partner to be an individual. Validation says something like, "It sounds as if your feelings have been deeply hurt;" or "It sounds as if you are very frustrated right now." Validation does not evaluate what your spouse believes or feels; validation accepts the feeling.

Validation can become tricky. At times a spouse feels offended when he or she has simply misunderstood what we said. We get accused of things we did not mean to do. And then we get caught up in the details of the accusations instead of the feelings. In turn we try to correct the faulty accusations, but our spouses often interpret this as defensiveness, argumentativeness, or invalidation.

One time Erin was describing an embarrassing moment that she felt I'd intentionally caused. I said, "I hear you saying that you felt embarrassed when I told that story in our small group last night, even though I had no idea that story bothered you. I've told it before, and you didn't seem to mind." Even though I was trying to validate her feeling of embarrassment, I was also trying to defend myself at the same time. Ultimately Erin did not feel validated. I walked away feeling that my intentions had been totally misunderstood. In hindsight, the better strategy would have been to first validate Erin's feelings and emotions. It's never a question of her feelings being right or wrong, even if she has misunderstood me. Remember, I can always give her a gift of feeling understood. After validating Erin's feelings, I would have had the opportunity to talk about my emotions of feeling misunderstood and wrongly accused.

Validation avoids this. It recognizes the pain and the hurt. It focuses on the emotion. It says, "It sounds as if your feelings were hurt. That was not my intention, but I obviously hurt you. So how can I make it right?" When you speak like this, you begin to validate your spouse.

Before we conclude this section, allow me to clarify something that can become a major obstacle when validating your spouse. It can be very hard to validate someone when you disagree with what the person is saying. When you believe what he or she is saying is incorrect, misleading, or inaccurate, it can feel very difficult to validate the person's feelings.

The key is to realize that validation has nothing to do with whether you agree or disagree with what the person is saying. You might totally disagree with what has been said. But you can always validate a person's thoughts, opinions, and feelings (especially their emotions), no matter what. So don't get caught up in this dangerous trap of thinking you have to agree with what is said. You'll have an opportunity later to provide your perspective when it's your turn to be the customer.

On several occasions Erin has talked about getting hurt by a female friend. As I have listened to her describe her pain and hurt, I have made the same mistake over and over again. Instead of validating her feelings, I often try to explain my perception of the event. I will usually assert that perhaps Erin misunderstood or misinterpreted the person's actions. The problem is that I violate the first rule of validation: I don't have to agree with her to validate her. Instead of encouraging Erin to see the flip side of the coin, I should just focus on her feelings and emotions.

So what do we really listen for during the validation process? We listen not only for emotions and feelings but also to understand the "nuggets"—the most important and deepest concerns of our spouse. Take a look.

Get to the Nugget

One aspect of this communication process provides the key to the whole thing. Picture LUV Talk to be like a funnel. The goal is to sift through a lot of material to funnel down to the absolute nugget, which is, "How did I feel *about myself?*"

If I go to the butcher and tell him, "I need a filet mignon," he may point to a big hunk of meat surrounded by three inches of fat. "I really don't want the fat," I say, and so he begins the process of trimming that hunk of meat down to the nugget I want, the filet mignon.

> **PROMISED LAND TIP**
> You do not have to agree with your spouse to validate him or her. Validation is simply listening to and trying to understand your spouse's deep emotions and feelings.

In the same way, you use LUV Talk to get to the nugget, the filet mignon—but first you have to trim away the fat. How? Every time you say back how your spouse felt, you try to get a little closer to his or her core feeling: how he felt about himself, how she felt about herself. It's like trimming away another layer of fat until the essence, the nugget, appears.

Some counselors advise couples to trade off between the customer and the employee before they reach this nugget, but I disagree. If you don't allow the customer to get to the nugget, it can be really hard to identify. So I encourage people to focus on the customer until they identify that person's nugget.

Once the customer finds the nugget, you trade places, and your spouse does the same thing for you. "It sounds like this is how you felt," you might say. "How did that make you feel about yourself?" You're not allowed to talk about yourself or defend yourself. And you're not allowed to make a list of comments that you plan to address later.

It makes all the difference when a spouse hangs in there long enough to get to the nugget. You see the lights going on when the listener says, "Is this it?" and the speaker replies, "Wow, that's *it!*"

At the end of this process you're left with two golden nuggets. Then, as a couple, you take those two nuggets and factor them both into your solution. That's how you get to a win-win solution.

A No-Losers Policy

Bob Paul has taught me a wonderful truth about relationships. In fact, what Bob developed in his family has had an incredibly positive impact in my marriage. It's called a no-losers policy. A no-losers policy simply means that there is no such thing as win-lose. We either have a lose-lose or a win-win. Since we're on the same team, we either win together or we lose together. If I take what is most important to you and you take what is most important to me and we add both into the mix, we always end up with a win-win solution. We must go into this process with this attitude: "We've created a no-losers policy. We're teammates. We're on the same team."

As a consequence, we will use this method to work out our differences. Ultimately, we're trying to walk through the doorway of intimacy—and we get to that doorway by digging out these nuggets.

The goal here is not simply to go back and forth to understand some general feelings; the goal is to truly understand something very specific, namely, this nugget. Unless we know that we're trying to draw out this nugget—the deepest need or concern—then we won't necessarily look for it.

Consider another medical analogy. Good physicians will always funnel down to the most important issues. They might hear a lot of peripheral things, but their goal is to be able to say, "Here are the three or four things that I really need to understand." Then, after hearing the answers to those three or four questions, they say, "Based on what I understand you to say, this is my diagnosis."

> **PROMISED LAND TIP**
> When solving conflicts, adopt the attitude that says the only acceptable solution is one that both people feel good about. Remember, as a team, you either win together or lose together. There is no other alternative.

That's what we need to do through LUV Talk. We need to be good physicians who get to the nugget that will enable us to make a proper diagnosis. "So it sounds as if this thing is really important to you," I might say. "If I'm hearing this right, it sounds as if you felt really frustrated, disappointed, and hurt that you weren't included in this discussion. That sounds as if it was really important to you."

"Yes."

"So if I'm hearing you right, this is the most important thing?"

"Absolutely."

By funneling to the nugget—in the case of the illustration, that the person felt hurt not to be included in the discussion—we experience a truly magical moment: "You really get me!"

There's nothing on earth like being "gotten." And that's what I find so remarkable about the LUV Talk method. With a little work, it regularly allows us to "get" each other. Even when the issue still feels raw.

Whose Bedroom Is It?

When Erin and I learned that we were expecting our son, Garrison, we lived in a house with three bedrooms and a loft. We already had two children, and Erin wanted every child to have his or her own bedroom. So we decided to remodel the loft into a fourth bedroom. We came up with a design, hired a remodeler to build it, and stood back to admire our new addition. As we scanned the newly finished room and its vaulted ceiling and spacious dimensions, we spoke almost simultaneously.

"All right!" Erin said. "Let's get the baby stuff up here."

"Finally!" I said. "Let's move Taylor in here."

We stopped, did a double take, looked at each other and asked, "What did you just say?"

"Let's get the baby stuff because this is going to be Garrison's room," Erin said.

"No, it's not," I replied. "This is Taylor's room. This is a really cool room."

"This isn't Taylor's room, it's Garrison's room!"

"This isn't Garrison's room, it's Taylor's room!"

We didn't have an all-out battle, but we both realized, *Well, I'll be. We have a difference of opinion about this.*

Over the next week or so, we tried to talk through this dilemma, but we got nowhere. Erin remained stuck on her idea, and I remained stuck on mine. We would argue about it and give each other all the reasons why we were right, but we never truly heard each other. So we stayed stuck, unable to make a decision.

Meanwhile, the loft room remained empty.

The situation quickly became very hurtful. Erin was starting to wonder, *What is your problem?* while I thought, *What is your problem?*

Without working through the conflict, we drove down to speak at a marriage seminar in Joplin, Missouri. It felt raw talking about the problem even in the car. At the seminar we had been scheduled to teach about LUV Talk, yet somehow we had never enlisted its help for this problem. In some ways, that's quite normal. Erin and I use some of these dance steps at some times and not at others. But if we really want to solve a problem, ultimately we have to use LUV Talk.

When Erin and I team-teach this method, we often write down on small pieces of paper four or five recent conflicts, put them into a basket, and let someone from the audience pick one. Then we demonstrate—live and in person—how the method works. As we got ready to go onstage, she asked, "Should we put in the one about the bedroom?"

"Not on your life," I replied. "We haven't figured this deal out."

For some reason she wrote it down anyway and sneaked it into the basket.

As we sat in front of about five hundred people, we sent the basket into the audience and asked someone to snag one of the five pieces of paper. You know which problem got picked, don't you? (I'm convinced that all five slips of paper said the same thing.)

So there I sat, in front of the crowd, beading up with sweat. *We're going to fail at this!* I thought, activating my fear button. We hadn't worked through this conflict, and I felt certain I would take a fall in front of everyone and end up looking like a moron. So I glared at Erin. She smiled back sweetly and actually said to the audience, "Greg asked me not to put this one in, but I did anyway because I wanted to show you how powerful this method is."

And I thought, *How could you?*

I took a deep breath and finally said, "Guys, you know what? I really believe in LUV Talk. I believe in it so much that I'm convinced with all my heart that we can actually do this. And she's right—we haven't worked through this issue yet."

> **PROMISED LAND TIP**
> Using LUV Talk can help you get to the most important needs or concerns—the nuggets. Those nuggets then become part of the win-win solution.

Even as I spoke, I realized, *I don't really have any opinions about this. I don't know why I'm so stuck.*

I turned to Erin and said, "You be the customer first!" So I took on the role of employee, the listener.

To shorten the story, as I began to listen and trim away the fat, we got to her nugget, her filet, the thing to which we were funneling: "I really need for us to be able to talk about what each child needs." In order to make a decision about the bedroom, Erin needed to talk about the needs of each child, and she didn't feel we had ever done that. So on her own she had thought through what each child needed, and she had concluded that Garrison had the most needs for that room.

Then we switched positions. At first I didn't know where this was going, but eventually it began to funnel, as it always does. It funneled beautifully, right down to my biggest issue: I did not feel that I had been included in the decision. I felt that Erin had determined on her own that Garrison needed the room. I thought, *So, I'm not even necessary?*

I then said, "The solution to our problem needs to contain both nuggets. We have to talk about each child's needs, and I have to feel included in the decision."

The audience loved it. Everyone could tell this was both real and raw. We hadn't drummed this up, and the crowd stayed right with us. We asked, "Okay, if these are our two nuggets, what do you think the solution could be?"

One guy stood up and said, "Hey, wipe the slate clean and incorporate both of your nuggets to reach a decision." We heard murmurs of approval throughout the audience: "Yeah, that's perfect. That will work. Good idea!"

Once we got home, it took us all of about ten minutes to reach a solution. We first set both of our previous solutions aside and started with a clean slate. We then made a list of every child's needs, realized that Garrison had some unique needs, and ultimately decided together that the room should be his. I felt included, the decision made sense to me, and that was it. *Finito.*

Although we ultimately settled on Erin's idea, we mutually adopted a win-win solution. I didn't "compromise" anything in the decision since we both got what we most wanted. And what could be sweeter than that?

RULE 4: RESOLUTION

The apostle Peter instructs us, "Finally, all of you, live in harmony with one another; be sympathetic, love as brothers, be compassionate and humble" (1 Peter 3:8, NIV). LUV Talk aims for win-win solutions to conflict, since no such thing exists as a win-lose arrangement. And you cannot resolve your conflicts until both of you completely understand each other's feelings and needs.

Couples usually argue about surface events such as cleaning, taking out the trash, where to go out at night, finances, disciplining the children—the list goes on and on. But beneath all such arguments lies something in common: the feelings and needs associated with the surface events. Couples spend decades arguing about the same thing because they never get to the feelings and needs underlying the conflict.

That is why we try to make sure that couples understand the feelings and needs that led to their conflict before they try to resolve it. How can we solve a conflict if we do not truly understand what it is about?

If you never go deeper than the surface event and continue to argue

> PROMISED LAND TIP
> Never move on to resolution until both people first feel heard and understood—validated.

about the event—and not the feelings and needs associated with the event—then you will find it extremely difficult to arrive at a win-win situation. If you want to plan a vacation, for example, and one of you wants to go to the beach while the other wants to snow ski, someone will obviously lose if you do not go deeper than the surface events (where to go). You can't go to the beach and snow ski at the same time. If you go deeper, however, and reach for feelings and needs, then you can reach a win-win solution.

After you have reached complete understanding of feelings and needs, then it's time to brainstorm all of the possible solutions to your conflict. Make sure this becomes a creative time and not a critical one. There are no bad ideas in a brainstorming session. If you evaluate or criticize a potential solution, you may find yourself right back in the middle of a heated conflict. Why risk it? You never know when a goofy idea might lead to a win-win solution!

After you have dreamed up all the possible solutions to your conflict, then it's time to start evaluating them and to pick a solution that works for both of you. Once you have agreed on a solution, live with it for a while and then come back together and reevaluate it. Force yourself to evaluate your solutions; this will give you the opportunity to modify the solution if your first idea didn't work the way you had hoped it would. Relationships are dynamic and continuously change with the tides of emotions and circumstances. You never have to stick with just one solution. Several solutions might work better than your original.

The point is that you are never done when it comes to your relationship. If you are not growing, you are dying. And LUV Talk is designed for the living.

NOTHING AS POWERFUL

I don't know of any other communication method as powerful as LUV Talk. Researchers have found that when you use LUV Talk, you eliminate relationship germs. You don't escalate, you don't withdraw, you don't belittle each other, and you don't form negative beliefs. If both partners follow the rules and create a safe zone for discussion, this thing *works*.

Nearly every time that Erin and I need to solve a persistent problem, we use LUV Talk. Of course, we've modified it over the years. We no longer have to follow the rules quite so rigidly as we did in the beginning. Back then, we applied the rules in an unbending way (and had to). Now we use a modified version. If I really

> **PROMISED LAND TIP**
> When starting to learn LUV Talk, do not begin with painful issues or highly sensitive subjects. Start with less volatile conflicts. Difficult subjects can derail the process at first. However, as your skills improve, you will begin to feel safe using LUV Talk with more serious and sensitive matters.

need to be understood, I'll say, "Can you repeat that to make sure that I know you understand?" Even in everyday conversation, when I want to help her know that I really "get" her, I'll say back what I hear her saying, focusing especially on the emotion.

Remember, LUV Talk is not the most complicated communication system in the world. If you can give an order at McDonald's, you can use LUV Talk to resolve all of your biggest conflicts.

One word of caution: I encourage you not to begin LUV Talk on a highly sensitive subject or a very hurtful area from your past. Start with less volatile conflicts, like being late for dinner. Difficult subjects can be troublesome at first. As your skills improve at using this life-changing method, you will begin to feel safe using it with more serious and sensitive matters. Take your time. Trust me, it works. It's been proven for years to be the most powerful communication method available.[5]

AND THAT WAS THAT

Remember the painful, four-year-long conflict Erin and I had over money? For those first forty-eight months of our marriage, we couldn't even discuss money without getting into a bitter argument.

And then we took a trip from L.A. to San Diego, where we learned the rudiments of LUV Talk. In a three-hour drive back home, we used the method to talk about this volatile issue—and resolved it before we walked in our front door.

That's how powerful LUV Talk is. Why not let it help you resolve your own conflicts?

SUMMARY OF LUV TALK RULES

EMPLOYEE (Listener)

* This person's job is to listen.
* Listen for the customer's feelings and emotions.
* When receiving an order, you must say back only what you've heard. No editing, evaluating, or defending yourself. You can ask to have the order repeated if you did not understand something, but this is only for clarity—you don't have to agree.

CUSTOMER (Speaker)

* This person's job is to share needs or feelings using "I" statements. No bringing up past issues, starting a new argument, or making "You" statements that blame the other (e.g., "You always . . .").
* The focus should be on the customer's feelings and emotions.
* Give bite-size pieces of information that the other person can remember easily. That way, he or she can repeat the information correctly.

GENERAL RULES

* Repeating statements does not mean you agree with what is being said. Instead, the goal is to listen and validate the person's feelings and individuality.
* When the customer feels heard and validated and you have captured the "nugget," then you switch places.
* You are not looking for solutions at this time. Solutions can be explored after each person feels heard and validated.
* Agree to take a time-out if withdrawal, escalation, invalidation, or negative beliefs creep into the conversation.
* Above all else, strive to honor one another in all that is said and repeated.

4

Entering the
Promised Land

CHAPTER 11

DEPENDING ON GOD'S POWER

But the Lord said to Joshua, "I have given you Jericho, its king, and all its mighty warriors. Your entire army is to march around the city once a day for six days. Seven priests will walk ahead of the Ark, each carrying a ram's horn. On the seventh day you are to march around the city seven times, with the priests blowing the horns. When you hear the priests give one long blast on the horns, have all the people give a mighty shout. Then the walls of the city will collapse, and the people can charge straight into the city."

JOSHUA 6:2-5

WHEN YOU NEED a radical change in your circumstances—when nothing less than a miracle will do—you need God. There are no substitutes.

A woman named Olga Avetisova lived out this principle a few years ago when she supervised a ministry of mercy in the prisons, labor camps, and institutions of Uzbekistan (a part of the former Soviet Union). A prison warden opposed Avetisova's work and barred any compassionate workers from passing inside the walls of her institution.

What could Avetisova do? She prayed and asked supporting congregations to join her, pleading with God to somehow knock down the walls. If anything positive was to happen, Avetisova knew that God had to intervene.

The Lord heard the prayers of his people and answered them decisively—but not at all in the way these faithful Christians expected. As God so often does, he intervened in a manner that no one could have predicted: a plane crash took the life of the antagonistic warden. And the woman's replacement? The new warden promptly opened the prison gates to Avetisova's colleagues.

"We didn't pray for her to die," Avetisova explained, "but that the door would be opened."[1]

LIVING INSIDE A MIRACLE

When an individual or a people accept God's invitation to partner with him, they shouldn't feel surprised to find themselves living inside a miracle. At Jericho, the people of God saw just how seriously the Lord takes this partnership.

Forty years had passed since the Israelites left slavery in Egypt. A new generation of Hebrews stood ready to accept God's call to enter the Promised Land. Yet an enormous obstacle blocked their way: Jericho, a large fortress city crammed with experienced warriors who were determined to crush the Israelites' advance. The looming walls of Jericho no doubt filled the Hebrews' hearts with dismay. What could God's people do?

They did what all sensible believers ought to do: They listened to God and followed his instructions. They were to march around the city for six days, led by seven priests carrying rams' horns and the Ark of the Covenant. On the seventh day they were to march around Jericho seven times with the priests blowing the horns. When the priests gave one long blast on the horns, the people were instructed to shout loudly. God promised that the walls of Jericho would collapse.

It sounds bizarre, doesn't it? No human general would have dreamed up such a strange plan. No military tactician would have thought to use an essentially religious ceremony to obliterate a strong city's defenses. Yet these Israelites had learned well their lessons in the wilderness. They had seen God work and had come to place their trust in him, no matter how odd some of his ways might seem. So they carefully followed the Lord's instructions—and watched him knock down the walls of Jericho. An excited General Joshua told his people, "Shout! For the Lord has given you the city!" (Joshua 6:16).

The thick walls of Jericho came down, not because of some amazing strategy dreamed up by the Israelites, but because they trusted God to accomplish what only he can do. The Hebrew nation gained entry into the Promised Land through a miracle—nothing less. The Israelites could have strapped on the finest armor, wielded the strongest swords, thrown the sharpest spears, and shot the deadliest arrows—and yet not made a dent in the ancient city's walls. But what they could not do, God did—in a unique, unorthodox, bizarre kind of way.

He likes to do that sort of thing.

THE GATEWAY TO THE PROMISED LAND

Only through Jericho did the Israelites gain access to the Promised Land. Only when God's people trusted him to do the impossible did they set foot in a countryside flowing with milk and honey.

I think each one of us needs to experience our own Jericho. What happened at Jericho provides the most important key to fully enjoying marriage as God intended. Jericho represents the last barrier that needs to be broken down before we can experience a Promised Land marriage. What is that barrier? Our stubborn will. We have to follow the Israelites' example and totally give ourselves over to God. We have to say, "God, I can't do this. You have to do it. So by faith, I'm asking you to do your thing."

When we relinquish control to God, he brings down the walls and paves the way for us to enter the Promised Land.

THE ROLE OF PRAYER

Perhaps more than any other activity, prayer reminds us that God is in charge and that we need his involvement to achieve true success. Whenever we pray, we acknowledge that we depend on God to do for us what we cannot do for ourselves.

And what does this have to do with marriage? You may not have heard the news, but recent studies reveal that couples who pray together every day have a divorce rate of *less than one percent.*[2]

Would you like to divorce-proof your marriage? Then make time every day to pray with your spouse. When you both come before a holy and loving God in a posture of trust and dependence, you invite him to accomplish in your marriage what only he can do. A husband and wife who commit themselves to the Lord in prayer know that they don't ultimately control their own lives. They also see each other regularly humbling themselves before God. How could such a couple not have a good relationship?

On the other hand, do you see how counterintuitive this seems? Who would think to name "daily prayer together" as an overwhelming indicator of successful marriage? Having fun together or planning together or significant conversations together or making financial decisions together—all of those things seem obvious. But daily *prayer* together? On a surface level, it seems to make little sense.

In God's world, however, the odd and the strange often become his chosen avenues to success. Why? Because these methods lift our eyes from ourselves and place them firmly on him. Through such "odd" means, God reminds us that he is the Almighty One and we are his dependent children. God brings down the walls in his unique way, whenever he chooses. Our job is to trust him, however unusual it might seem at the time.

PROMISED LAND TIP
Couples who pray together every day have a divorce rate that is less than 1 percent. Pray together every day!

THE DESTRUCTION OF SELF-WILL

For marriage, Jericho symbolizes the destruction of our self-will. True freedom comes as the result of God's efforts, not our own. While we cannot defeat our fears, God can.

Scripture says that God is love (see 1 John 4:16). It also says that perfect love casts out all fear (see 1 John 4:18). When we submit to God and depend on him, we can tap his limitless resources to render our fears powerless. When we do things our way and refuse to depend on God, however, then our Jerichos will continue to stand. It's either God's way or our way.

I admit, of course, that allowing God to be in control of our marriage is easier said than done. Even so, sometimes we have no choice but to completely submit to God. And at that moment God does wonders in our relationship.

How can I forget the time that I lost total control and *had* to submit to God? It happened the day Erin almost died.

"There is something wrong with you," I said to Erin in a panic. "I'm taking you to the hospital." So we rushed to the emergency room.

At the time Erin was thirty-eight weeks pregnant with our middle child, Maddy. My wife hadn't felt well for several weeks; she could push her finger in the swollen flesh of her ankles and leave a crater-sized pit. She had other symptoms as well, but none of them gave us any clue about what lay in store for us.

At the hospital, nurses hooked Erin up to monitors, and doctors ran various tests. Finally, they diagnosed Erin with an extremely dangerous condition called HELLP syndrome, a lethal form of toxemia.[3] Essentially the baby becomes toxic to the mother's body. As the woman's body fights against the baby, she can develop multiple organ damage. Symptoms include high blood pressure, pitting edema (causing the crater-sized pits in her ankles), visual problems, stomach pains, and impaired liver function. The mom may develop seizures, slip into a coma, or even die. Erin was in extreme danger!

The moment the doctors realized the problem, they rushed to perform an emergency cesarean section. I had only minutes to understand the situation. While I ran down the hallway, trying to get dressed in surgical scrubs, the nurse started telling me what was happening. I heard little of her explanation regarding

HELLP except for one thing: I heard her say the words "possibility of death."

Death! Did that nurse just say that Erin could *die?*

I never felt more scared and helpless than I did that day. As I watched the doctors perform the emergency C-section, I could do nothing but submit to God.

"What do you mean," you might be asking, "that all you could do was to give control over to God? That was a no-brainer!"

Perhaps. But remember that my fear button is failure. I try to guard against failure by being in control. I try to be self-sufficient so I can control the outcome. Obviously, this never works. Nevertheless, I like to take control since the illusion of control gives me a false sense of security—and even a false sense of security sometimes feels better than no security. While I know that my ultimate security comes from God's being in control, it's not always easy for me to relinquish control to him. I still struggle with seizing back control of my life.

On that day, however, I could do nothing. I was completely helpless. Still, a tremendous sense of peace washed over me because I knew that God was in control. That knowledge gave me peace because I believed what the apostle Paul had written: "Since God did not spare even his own Son but gave him up for us all, won't God, who gave us Christ, also give us everything else?" (Romans 8:32).

I didn't know how things would turn out, but I knew that God was in charge. The more I prayed and released control, the more secure I felt.

As terrible as HELLP can be, at least it ends once the baby leaves the mother's body. In most cases, the mother and child quickly move out of danger. Thank God that's what happened with Erin and Maddy. In a few hours Erin's physical condition stabilized and improved.

Many weeks after Maddy's delivery, I learned that at the exact moment I was releasing control to Christ, Erin was singing words to a popular Christian song—"Yes, Lord, yes, Lord, yes, yes, Lord"—her way of releasing her life to Christ.

I still struggle every day with submitting my will to God. But Erin and I use her story as a battle cry to remember that we must submit to God and allow him to be in control. When that happens, our relationship is never better.

I'm amazed by the correlation between a satisfying marriage and dependence on God. It seems that the more Erin and I submit to God and allow him to control our relationship, the happier we feel and the more satisfying our relationship becomes. That doesn't necessarily mean we have less conflict or fewer problems! But when those conflicts and problems occur, we tap into the One with all the power necessary to overcome them.

A FEW QUICK REMINDERS

Why is conscious, willing dependence on God so crucial to achieving a Promised Land marriage? Let's remind ourselves of a few basics.

We Are Created for Relationship

God created us as relational beings, first and foremost to be in relationship with himself. "So God created people in his own image," the Bible says. "God patterned them after himself; male and female he created them" (Genesis 1:27).

God didn't create us to be like him so much as he created us to relate to him. God also created us to be in relationship with others. He himself declared that it was "not good" for the first man, Adam, to be "alone" (even though God was with Adam from the beginning). Therefore God created a way for us to be in relationship with others (see Genesis 2:18, 20-24).

When someone asked Jesus to name the most important commandment, he replied, "The most important commandment is this: 'Hear, O Israel! The Lord our God is the one and only Lord. And you must love the Lord your God with all your heart, all your soul, all your mind, and all your strength.' The second is equally important: 'Love your neighbor as yourself.' No other commandment is greater than these" (Mark 12:29-31). Jesus makes it clear that the Lord created us to be in relationship with God, self, and others.

We Are Created to Depend on God

God placed Adam in Paradise and supplied him with everything he needed (see Genesis 2:8-10). God also made it possible for Adam to have an everlasting relationship with his Creator. God clearly created Adam a dependent creature. Humankind was not supposed to live apart from God, to be autonomous or self-sustaining. God did not intend Adam and Eve to gain eternal life, wisdom, or even their basic physical needs apart from him. God created us to depend on him.

We Are Made with the Capacity to Choose

In the middle of the Garden, God placed two trees: the tree of life and the tree of the knowledge of good and evil. The fruit of the tree of life gave the eater everlasting life, a godlike quality. The fruit of the tree of the knowledge of good and evil gave the eater wisdom to know good and evil, also a godlike quality.

While God created us to depend on him, he also gave us free will, the ability to choose. If God had wanted a dependent humanity without free will, then why would he have placed the two trees—trees whose fruit, when eaten, would result in independence from God—within our grasp? God intentionally created a dependent human race with the capacity to choose.

We Are to Freely Choose to Depend on God

God wants us to *choose* to depend on him. He desires that we willingly place our trust in him to sustain our lives. Although in a larger sense we remain dependent on God regardless of what we choose—as Job says, "In his hand is the life of every creature and the breath of all mankind" (Job 12:10, NIV)—yet the Lord wants us to freely give up control of our lives to him. He wants to guide us and direct us toward the best possible road, and he wants us to willingly follow his lead (see Psalm 32:8-9).

Ultimately, God wants us to return to his original pattern, in which Adam lived in an unspoiled Eden. He wants us to freely choose to depend on him so that he may provide us with all the resources we need.

When Adam and Eve chose to take control of their own lives and spurned God's direction, their foolish actions separated them from God. What they feared the most—loss of relationship—came to pass when they chose to become independent by controlling their own lives.

We Have a Way to Get Reconnected

Ever since Adam and Eve chose to disobey God, humankind has suffered separation from God. As a consequence, we've tried to be self-sufficient. But this has not worked; we continue to fail at relationships.

Remember the statistic quoted earlier that among the 50 percent of couples who remain married, only 25 percent of those say they feel satisfied? That means that only about 12 percent experience satisfaction. It appears that the other 88 percent either end up divorced, separated, or living in the wilderness.

I wonder how many marriages become truly Promised Land relationships. My guess is, not very many. Why not? We try to have a great marriage our way, not God's way. Yet we can never have a Promised Land marriage our way. We can, however, have such a marriage through God!

In love, our merciful God designed a way for us to regain connection with him. When we place our faith in his crucified and risen Son, Jesus Christ, we gain eternal life and an intimate connection with him. The moment we give up control of our lives and depend totally on Christ to be our Lord, we start to reap all the tremendous benefits that a divine connection implies.

It's funny, but the very thing that Eve refused to give up—control—is the very thing we have to give up if we want to get reconnected with God. In that way the story comes full circle.

THE DIFFICULTY OF SURRENDER

So, is it easy to give up control? You already know the answer to that! Ever since the fall of Adam and Eve, human beings have naturally craved independence and self-sufficiency. We want to remain in control. Even though it doesn't work, even though this grasping for control undermines and sabotages our most cherished relationships, we persist in our independent ways. In the marriage intensives at the Smalley Marriage Institute we see this scenario played out repeatedly.

By the afternoon of the second day, the control issue normally takes the floor. We do our best to explain the Jericho stage of the journey and challenge the couples to give up control to God.

That's when the real battle begins.

Almost always we encounter immediate and strong resistance. These husbands and wives have worked to keep control for so long that to give it up seems like madness. So we hammer at their resistance and remind them of specific incidents that show how their attempts to seize control have done nothing but hurt their relationship (the Fear Dance). After a pitched struggle, most of these couples eventually give up and say, in essence, "You know what? I can't defend against this anymore." By that point they have little choice but to say, "Okay, God, I give up. I can't do this. I can't fix my marriage. I can't change the Fear Dance. You have to do it."

And at that moment, we watch a miracle. The walls come down!

We normally see this happen several times each month. When a husband and wife reach Jericho, a remarkable transformation occurs. They give God control, he provides the resources and the method to bring down their walls, and a shout of victory goes up from the surprised and elated camp.

I've watched Jericho happen in my own life. Even after Erin

PROMISED LAND TIP
Our walls will come down not from our effort but through God's efforts.

and I had identified our Fear Dance and spent a lot of time talking about it, for a while we allowed it to continue to hurt our relationship. Just knowing about the Fear Dance doesn't make it go away. Not until we both said, "We can't do this on our own. God, you have to do it," did we begin to enjoy real progress.

There simply aren't enough skills to enable us to overcome the inertia of our fallen nature and the power of our Fear Dance. Skills don't have the muscle to clear a path for us into the Promised Land. Skills can prepare us for success and bring us to a spot where God can use such tools effectively, but ultimately, only God can bring us into the Promised Land.

I wonder what it would look like in your life to give God control of your marriage. What needs to happen so that the Lord can supply all the resources you need? What might need to change in your marriage so that he's the one calling the shots?

THE PLACE OF BOUNDARIES

Relinquishing control to God scares most of us to death. We can't help but wonder, *What if I give him control, and I get hurt? What if I surrender to his will, and my spouse sticks a dagger in my heart?*

My colleague Bob Paul early on recognized this common fear. Therefore he developed some guidelines for creating healthy boundaries within relationships.

I believe a lot of people have the wrong idea about boundaries. They think of a boundary as a wall, an armed fortress that they create around their hearts so that they don't get hurt. When people start to wound them, they pull back and set a boundary that affords them some protection.

Bob doesn't see boundaries in that way. His unique take on the nature of boundaries has helped me personally a great deal.

Bob insists that God created us to channel his love to others. Of course, we can choose to shut down that flow. We can close off the process, build a dam. But God doesn't want that to happen.

PROMISED LAND TIP
The goal of a boundary is to keep your heart open to others.

Our goal, Bob says, ought to be not walls around our hearts, but open hearts. The goal can't be protection from others, but ministry to others. The boundaries we establish should enable us to keep our hearts open, not to close them off. Relinquishing control to God enables us to keep our hearts open so that the Lord can use us to have an impact on others. We'll never keep our hearts open, however, unless we first relinquish control.

If our spouses do something hurtful and we feel frustrated and wounded, then we are right to put a boundary in place. Even so, we ought to pull back just enough so that our hearts don't close off. Boundaries are really about regulating an open heart.

Perhaps you feel like one of the monkeys at a local zoo. "That's unbelievable, having a lion and a monkey in the same cage," said a visitor to the zookeeper. "How do they get along?"

"Pretty well, usually," replied the zookeeper. "Occasionally they have a disagreement, and we have to get a new monkey."

You may feel that each time you get into a disagreement, your spouse comes down on you like a roaring lion. Perhaps you feel wounded or, like one of those monkeys, your spirit has been "killed." This is why setting boundaries in a marriage is so important. The last thing we want to do is to allow our spirits to close or get "killed off."

Boundaries allow our hearts to remain open. If during conflict or a heated discussion angry words or sarcastic statements fly, then call a time-out (take a break for at least twenty minutes). You are not withdrawing by doing this. Instead, you are keeping your heart open. You are actually loving your spouse enough to refuse to allow escalation to damage your relationship. Don't allow your heart to close or to become hardened. A boundary in your marriage is whatever you need to keep your heart open.

Where does this apply in your relationship?

In our marriage, Erin and I have had to protect our fun time.

We consider this one of the most important boundaries we've established. And we learned how to protect fun experiences the hard way.

Recently Erin and I planned to spend a day at Disneyland. Before entering the park, we decided to save money by eating at a nearby sandwich place. While I stuffed my mouth with a foot-long sub, I brought up a very sensitive issue, and an argument erupted. As the conflict escalated, we moved our "discussion" to the car, hoping to resolve the dispute without involving the entire restaurant. Unfortunately, the privacy didn't help.

Having no desire to spend the day walking around "the happiest place on earth" together, we drove home in silence. It took the entire day to resolve the argument, and in this way we ruined our Disneyland date.

Erin and I did what no married couple should ever do; we allowed conflict to infiltrate our enjoyment. When conflict or sensitive issues invade our recreation, it's like throwing a red shirt into the washer with our white clothes. Even though it's only one small shirt, it can color an entire load of laundry an ugly shade of pink. Likewise, even though you may plan to discuss only one tiny issue, the conflict can damage your entire experience. In this way, hurt can build, and hearts can close.

Conflict can cripple your recreation because it intensifies emotions; and as this happens, it becomes difficult to relax and enjoy each other. If this pattern occurs too often, your spouse may lose the desire to do fun things because the experience too often ends up "turning pink." When Erin and I started to argue in the restaurant, we should have done something to stop the process. Instead of allowing anger and hurt feelings to take over, we needed to set a boundary by calling a time-out.

Before conflicts destroy your enjoyment, I encourage you to interrupt arguments or sensitive discussions by setting a boundary. Agree to talk about the issue at a different time. Reschedule the conversation when you can provide the necessary attention it deserves. By setting the boundary and not allowing conflict to harm your recreation, you send a very important message: that protecting your relationship is more important than arguing about a problem.

Extend this image of boundaries and an open heart to think about a real heart. A human heart must have walls to function—but why does the heart exist? What is its purpose? It exists not to keep stuff out but to keep the rest of the body healthy by pumping oxygenated blood outside of itself. Its "boundaries" exist to benefit surrounding organs and tissue.

In the same way, God wants to work through us to minister to others. Therefore any boundaries that we put into place ought to serve that purpose. If we try to erect boundaries that work against that purpose—if we try to seize control back from God in an effort to protect ourselves—we plug up the heart. We crimp the hose. And as a consequence, the flow of blood gets cut off, not only to others, but also to ourselves.

Much better to keep the blood flowing!

A SAILBOAT, NOT A MOTORBOAT

The Smalley clan loves word pictures, and I'm no exception. If the image of an open heart doesn't help you to grasp what it means to relinquish control to God, maybe a nautical image will.

A friend, Dr. Jeff Fray, recently said that we are to be like a sailboat, not a motorboat. Our sails should remain wide open so that the wind of God's power can move us wherever he wants us to go. Think of God's invisible hand on the tiller; your job is to keep the sails in a position to catch the wind, not to steer the boat where you think it should go.

Naturally, we can't be passive in this process. While we neither steer nor motor the boat, we do manage its sails and keep them in good repair. When we manage the sails responsibly, we allow God to fill them with wind and manage the tiller however he sees fit. In that way we go wherever he chooses. If we fail to take care of the sails, if we allow holes to shred the fabric, then we can become totally ineffective for God. He can still use us, of course, but the voyage will go a lot smoother if we keep the equipment in top shape.

Are you effectively managing the sails of your boat? Or are you trying to maneuver a motorboat through high seas while angry waves pummel your sinking craft? If you're not sure, then ask your spouse. If you find your ship listing heavily to port, then I strongly recommend that you learn from a woman who has traded in her battered, old motor for a strong, beautiful sail.

"MY ISSUE IS CONTROL"

Some time ago a couple on the brink of divorce came to the Smalley Marriage Institute to participate in a marriage intensive. The wife was argumentative, boisterous, loud, demanding. Without question, this woman's issue came down to control. She coped with her fear of helplessness through large doses of aggression. She sought control in every aspect of her life. In fact, she came to the Institute with divorce papers literally in hand. On the first day, she walked into the room carrying a folder, the contents of which she revealed within the first hour.

"Here are the divorce papers," she said. "All I have to do is sign them to get the process under way." No doubt she already had scoped out the nearest post office.

In the process of the intensive, the Lord worked a miracle in her life. For the first time, she understood that she had to give up control to God. Throughout her married life she had focused intensely on her husband. But in those few days, she took personal responsibility and started putting into practice all of the skills we've been considering. At the end of the intensive she wept openly, a powerful moment for all of us.

"My marriage is saved," she sobbed. "Now I understand."

A month later she sent us a letter, written from the perspective of her five-year-old daughter—the spitting image of her mom. The letter listed all of the positive changes the little girl had noted in her mom and dad, and it thanked us for our help.

Within a few days we got a phone call from this woman. She wanted to know if we had received the letter. I told her we had.

"I have to tell you a funny story," she said. "You know how my issue was control?"

"Yes."

"You know how I get when I want control? I attack people."

"Yes."

"As you probably know, I spent a lot of time working on that letter."

"I know. It was a neat letter. I could tell that it took a lot of time."

She then explained how the mail carriers in her area had planned to go on strike, but for some reason they couldn't. So in a very passive-aggressive manner, they began leaving bundles of mail under bridges and in parking lots, just dumping letters to send the message that while they may not have been able to strike, they could disrupt the flow of mail. Citizens became extremely upset because they never knew what was being received and what wasn't. So when this woman's mail carrier approached her house, she confronted him.

"Listen!" she said, handing him the letter. "*Under no circumstances* are you allowed to put this under some bridge." She emotionally and verbally attacked him. She could sense that her attack had hurt him, but so what? She let him walk away, wounded and bleeding.

"Greg," she told me, "at that moment I realized that I was not letting God be in control; *I* was trying to control. So I prayed, 'God, you know what? You can deliver this letter if you want. And if it doesn't arrive, it doesn't arrive. I can't control this.' "

Without warning, a new impulse struck her: she felt compelled to humble herself and track down the man in order to deliver an apology. As she walked briskly down the street, the mail carrier saw her coming and immediately started to cower (probably while reaching for his pepper spray).

"Listen," she said, "this may sound really odd to you, but I struggle with needing to control everything, and I attack people when I don't feel as if I'm in control. I attacked you because I really wanted you to send this letter. But you know what I realized? I'm not in control. And that's okay. God's in control. And I just want you to know how sorry I am that I treated you this way because you are worth much more than that. I shouldn't have treated you so badly."

Her sincere apology opened the door to an ongoing conversation. A few days later the mail carrier began asking some pointed questions about spiritual things. Ultimately she helped the man become a Christian.

What might have happened had this woman continued to move to the harsh rhythms of her old dance? Where would that man be today if she had refused to give up control to God? What if he had subsequently seen her reading the Bible and thought, *How typical! What hypocrites those Christians are!* Who knows?

But because she relinquished control to God, she became an open vessel available for God to use. The Lord could have used anybody to reach that man with the good news of Jesus Christ, but he used this woman in that moment to speak to that guy—and her willing submission led to a decision with eternal consequences.

Yes, in this chapter we're still talking about marriage. But the story illustrates that by giving up control to God, you affect vastly more than your individual marriage.

God wants us to be in a place of total submission to him. If we want to get to the Promised Land, we have to give up control. We must go to Jericho and let God do his thing. He may use unorthodox and even bizarre methods to bring the walls down, but he'll do it.

> **PROMISED LAND TIP**
> When we relinquish control of our lives to God, we become open vessels for him to use.

And then the Promised Land can be ours.

CHAPTER 12

WHAT IS YOUR DREAM?

Stay on the path that the Lord your God has commanded you to follow. Then you will live long and prosperous lives in the land you are about to enter and occupy.

DEUTERONOMY 5:33

So what is it like once you reach the Promised Land? After Erin and I reached the Promised Land, we *never* had another fight! As soon as my wife and I made it past Jericho, we said, "Good-bye and good riddance!" to all our problems! These days, the sun never sets on our property, the rain always falls softly at night, and we never consume anything but milk and honey!

Can you tell that I'm joking?

The truth is, a Promised Land marriage is *not* a heavenly marriage. Why not? Achieving a Promised Land marriage doesn't mean that you have solved all your problems and therefore can avoid all further conflicts. What it does mean is that God will enable you to make your marriage the best it can be on this fallen planet of ours.

Unfortunately, we all have our fear buttons. Even after you settle down in the Promised Land, you'll still have fears. You'll still have lots of problems. And you'll still have to work through conflict. I daresay that some of your conflicts will look much as they did at the beginning of your relationship. What changes is not their existence but the way you deal with them.

THE SAME OLD FEARS

I vividly remember the countless times during our dating years that Erin and I stayed up until one or two in the morning, talking on the phone. On several occasions, I actually fell asleep during the conversation.

One time in particular, Erin was describing some of her frustrations with our relationship. While I valued her perspective, I just couldn't stay awake. As she continued to speak for an extended period, I interrupted her with incoherent ramblings about toothpaste, frozen pizza, and basketball.

The funniest part of the incident had nothing to do with what I said in my slumber. What I found hilarious was that Erin never realized I was talking in my sleep! Therefore she earnestly tried to debate my babble in the context of her concerns.

"See," she finally cried, "you *don't* care about me! All you care about is food and playing basketball!" I'm sure she had no idea about how to include the toothpaste into her accusations.

After several minutes of silence from me, Erin hung up the phone while yelling, "Fine! If you have nothing to say, if you're just going to withdraw into silence—then I'll hang up!"

If only I were a snorer, everything would have been fine. My first snort would have alerted her that I really wasn't giving her the silent treatment, just the REM treatment.

To make matters worse, I woke up the next morning with the phone still pressed against my ear. When I looked in the mirror, I had a digital version of the "mark of the beast" engraved on the side of my head, which read *AT&T*.

Although I no longer fall asleep on the phone while talking to my dear wife, I still sometimes struggle with actively listening to her. My failure to listen as I should occasionally leads us to conflict. But these days, when conflicts arise, we have the skills and the experience to deal with them more wisely. More important, we try to make surrendering to God a daily (if not hourly) experience. I always get into trouble when I try to rely on my own resources. The difference between having a good marriage (wilderness) and a great marriage (Promised Land) is surrendering to God. In surrendering, he will give us the power and the resources to make wise decisions in our marriage. Perhaps that's why I can't recall waking up ever again with a corporate brand on my temple.

TESTING HEARTS

Why does God permit our old fears to remain? Why doesn't he sweep them away the moment we give him control? I think our old fear buttons remain for the same reason that ancient Israel had to battle pagan enemies even after entering the Promised Land.

The book of Judges explicitly tells us that God left some of Israel's enemies in the Promised Land to test his people's hearts to see whether they would remain totally his. God said of these pagan nations, "I did this to test Israel—to see whether or not they would obey the Lord as their ancestors did" (Judges 2:22).

> **PROMISED LAND TIP**
> You will still have conflict in the Promised Land. Will you fall back into your Fear Dance, or will you choose to practice the new dance steps?

Just because Israel had entered the Promised Land didn't mean that all conflicts ceased. The book of Joshua describes how the nation went from battle to battle. When the Israelites obeyed God and allowed him to remain in control, they won. When they disobeyed God and took back control, they lost.[1]

Still, the longer the Israelites remained in the land, the more territory they conquered. And the more territory they controlled, the more Canaan became the righteous place—flowing with milk and honey—that God had envisioned long before.

WONDERFUL, NOT PERFECT

It seems to me that a Promised Land marriage has a lot in common with what confronted Joshua and the people of Israel. The Promised Land is not heaven; it's wonderful, but not perfect.

Just as God left enemies in the land to test Israel, so he leaves our fear buttons in place to test us. Will we continue to trust him, even when those old enemies cause us problems? When we get good at managing our fears, will we continue to depend on the Lord?

The Fear Dance doesn't end for good just because we've passed through Jericho. At the same time, however, the Fear Dance doesn't have to yank us back to Egypt. With God's help, we can avoid the unhealthy practices that kept us stuck in misery and practice the dance steps we learned in the wilderness.

Those skills come with us to the Promised Land. We need to see them as battle armor and as offensive gear to fight effectively in the fertile land God gives to us. Think of active listening as a sword, or think of honor as a shield. It might not hurt to spend some time working out for yourself a few wartime analogies that make sense to you. If you can connect these skills to an easily remembered picture, you'll be more likely to use them in a time of battle.

PICTURING YOUR OWN PROMISED LAND

As you continue on your journey, I want you to be clear about how you picture your own Promised Land marriage. You have enough information by this point to have an idea of where you'd like to end up. I'd like to give you an opportunity to cast a vision for your relationship. What is your dream for your marriage?

It may be that you're reading this book while you are still stuck in misery. Or perhaps you've just escaped from Egypt and feel as if you're floundering in the wilderness. That's okay. Wherever you are on your journey, the following exercise can give you a powerfully motivational picture of what life could be like for you in the Promised Land. You're more likely to keep moving ahead when you have a good idea of where you're headed.

When you and your spouse sit down *together* to develop a clear picture of what your Promised Land might look like, you'll have a concrete goal to move toward. And when you begin with a desired end in mind, you'll be far more likely to reach the destination of your dreams.

PROMISED LAND TIP
The Promised Land represents all that God intended marriage to be. It's your dream relationship.

I'd like to assist you in thinking through a few of the most important areas in any marriage. The following questions are designed to help you develop a clearer picture of what your own Promised Land marriage might look like.

- What is the vision of your ideal relationship?
- What does your Promised Land relationship look like?
- What positive things in the past helped you to have a great relationship?
- What are your marriage goals?
- How do you behave toward one another?
- What relational skills will you use in the Promised Land?
- How do you communicate love? How do you need your spouse to communicate love to you?
- If things were ideal in your marriage—if things were a ten—what would it look like?
- Complete the statement: "I feel loved when you . . ."
- How will you continue surrendering to God on a daily basis?
- Are you helping other couples to reach their Promised Land marriage?

MARRIAGE PURPOSE STATEMENT

What is a purpose statement? A purpose statement is a powerful document that expresses your personal sense of purpose and meaning in life; it acts as a governing constitution by which you evaluate decisions and choose behaviors.

Creating a marriage purpose statement will benefit you in a variety of ways:

- Helps your marriage to "begin with the end in mind"
- Encourages you to think deeply about your life
- Helps you examine your innermost thoughts and feelings
- Clarifies what is really important to you
- Expands your perspective
- Imprints self-determined values and purposes firmly in your mind
- Provides direction and commitment to values
- Enables you to make daily progress toward long-term goals
- Provides a mental creation of your desired results for your life and marriage

You can create your own marriage purpose statement by exploring what your marriage is all about and what principles you choose to guide your life. The goal here is to get both spouse's feelings and ideas out on the table. Answer these kinds of questions:

- What is the purpose of our marriage?
- What kind of marriage partners do we want to be?
- How do we want to resolve our differences?
- How do we want to handle our finances?
- What are our responsibilities as marriage partners?
- What are the principles and guidelines we want our marriage to follow?
- Who are our heroes? What is it about them that we like and would like to emulate?
- What marriages inspire us and why do we admire them?
- What roles (earning, financial management, housekeeping, and so on) will each of us have?

If you have children and if they are old enough to be part of a discussion about your family, invite them to answer some of these with you:

- What kind of parents do we want to be?
- What kind of family do we want to be?
- What kinds of things do we want to do?
- What kind of feeling do we want to have in our home?
- What kind of relationships do we want to have with one another?
- How do we want to treat one another and speak to one another?
- What things are truly important to us as a family?
- What are our family's priority goals?
- What are the unique talents, gifts, and abilities of our family members?
- How can we become a service-oriented couple and family?
- What traditions do we want to keep from our families of origin, and what new traditions do we want to create?
- How can we best relate to each other's families?

With ideas out on the table, you're now ready to refine, distill, and pull them all together into some kind of expression that will reflect the collective feeling of the hearts and minds of those who have contributed. Write a purpose statement that includes both your marriage and your family, if you have children. Consider the following example:

The purpose of our family is to create a nurturing place of faith, order, truth, love, happiness, and relaxation, and to provide opportunity for each individual to become responsibly independent and effectively interdependent in order to serve worthy purposes in society.

Our Marriage Purpose:

To love each other . . .
To help each other . . .
To believe in each other . . .
To wisely use our time, talents,
and resources to bless others . . .
To worship together . . .
Forever.

Our home will be a place where our family, friends, and guests find joy, comfort, peace, and happiness. We will seek to create a clean and orderly environment that is livable and comfortable. We will exercise wisdom in what we choose to eat, read, see, and do at home. We want to teach our children to love, learn, laugh, and to work and develop their unique talents.

WAKING UP TO REALITY

Now that you have a clearer idea of what your Promised Land might look like, allow me to let you in on a little secret: *The real thing will be a lot better than anything you can imagine.*

If you were to ask a little boy to name the best thing in the world, he might tell you, "A vanilla ice cream cone!" And a vanilla ice cream cone is great. But if you were to ask that same kid the identical question thirty years later, you'd almost certainly get a much different answer. Why? Because as we mature, our idea of "great" rises to higher levels, based on an expanded storehouse of information and a larger field of experience.

You have just developed an appealing picture of your own marriage that should help you to keep marching toward the Promised Land. But you know what? God wants to do something in your marriage far better than anything you can imagine. You're thinking about reaching Jupiter, and he's got a whole different galaxy in mind. Believe me, Promised Land marriage really can be great, fantastic, marvelous, the best experience on earth. I know hundreds of couples who have discovered that their experience of the Promised Land is actually far better than anything they could have imagined.

Yes, Promised Land marriage can be great, fantastic, marvelous, the best experience on earth. But it's still on earth, and that means that even the blessed calm can be shattered without a moment's notice.

When our older daughter, Taylor, was four months old, Erin and I had yet to learn about childproofing our home. I had a great stereo system that featured all the fancy options—you could program the unit to play for a couple of hours and then shut itself off, or you could have it wake you up with soothing music at seven o'clock in the morning. I loved it.

One evening I noticed Taylor fiddling with the stereo. Immediately I moved her away from it. But no matter what I did, she kept returning to it, like a moth to a flame. Finally we put her to bed. Shortly thereafter we went upstairs and went to bed too.

About two o'clock in the morning the freakiest noise I'd ever heard jolted us out of a deep slumber. The deafening beat of heavy metal rock exploded throughout our apartment. You know how it is when you're suddenly awakened from a dead sleep? The blaring music overloaded my senses and frightened me. I couldn't get my bearings. I didn't know where I was, and I couldn't figure out what was happening. All I knew was that the awful noise came from downstairs.

"We're being robbed!" Erin shouted. "You have to go down there!"

And I thought, *Yeah, right.*

I don't think I've ever felt quite so terrified in my life. The only light switch for downstairs was downstairs, so I had to descend in darkness into this throbbing, hellish abyss. I just *knew* that some criminal was hiding down there, waiting for me. I thought my heart would beat out of my chest.

It turned out, as you have guessed, that Taylor had cranked up the stereo all the way. She'd also somehow managed to set its alarm function for 2:00 A.M. (At dawn we began to educate ourselves about proper childproofing procedures.)

Life can be like that on a fallen planet. One moment you're dreaming peacefully in a gentle land flowing with milk and honey, and the next you're trying to evict a roomful of eardrum-fracturing, heavy metal fiends from your living room.

Is married life perfect in the Promised Land? No. But if you and your spouse intentionally partner with God to make your marriage all it can be on this earth, you'll have all the resources you need to quiet the din and get back to the business of delightful living.

Does that sound like a fantasy? Does that sound like a too-good-to-be-true dream? Does a Promised Land marriage sound like something possible only in the Bible and not in the real world where you live? If so, all I can say is that I know the dream of a Promised Land marriage *already has come true* for many couples, even for those who not long ago seemed destined for the divorce courts. As I've noted several times already, more than 90 percent of the at-risk couples who have visited us at the Smalley Marriage Institute are now either living in or traveling toward their own marital Promised Land. In a future book, I plan to invite readers to follow four couples through an actual marriage intensive, where they will learn the secrets of making real change take place in the most desperate of situations.

But for now, let me say it one last time: *You, too, can have a Promised Land marriage. You, too, can achieve the marriage of your dreams.* And when you do, you'll be able to join the psalmist in this most pleasant of songs:

I will lie down in peace and sleep,
for you alone, O Lord, will keep me safe. (Psalm 4:8)

IDENTIFYING YOUR FEAR DANCE

1. Describe a recent conflict or negative situation with your spouse—something that really "pushed your button." For the purpose of this exercise, be sure that you and your spouse write down the *same conflict*.

_____

_____

_____

_____

_____

2. How did this conflict make you feel about *yourself*? What did the conflict say about *you*? What was the *"self"* message—the message that it sent to *you*? What were the *buttons* that got pushed? Look through the options and use them to fill in the blanks in this statement: As a result of the above conflict, I felt _____ or feared feeling _____. Check all that apply—but "star" the most important feeling:

✓ or *	"As a result of the conflict, I felt . . ."	What That Feeling Sounds Like
	Rejected	I will be discarded; I will be seen as useless; my spouse doesn't need me; I am not necessary in this relationship; my spouse doesn't desire intimacy with me.
	Unwanted	My spouse doesn't want me; my mate will not choose me; my spouse is staying in the marriage out of duty, obligation, or because it's the "right" thing to do.
	Abandoned	I will be alone; my spouse will ultimately leave me; my spouse won't be committed to me for life.
	Disconnected	We will become emotionally detached or separated; there are walls or barriers between us in the marriage.
	Like a failure	I am not successful at being a husband/wife; I will not perform right or correctly; I will fall short in my relationship; I won't make the grade.
	Helpless or powerless	I cannot do anything to change my spouse or my situation; I do not possess the power, resources, capacity, or ability to get what I want.
	Controlled	I will be controlled by my spouse; my mate will exercise authority over me; I will be made to "submit"; my spouse will restrain me; I will be treated like a child or my mate will act like my parent.
	Defective	Something is wrong with me; I'm the problem; I am unlovable.
	Inadequate	I am not capable; I am incompetent.
	Inferior	Everyone else is better than I am; I am less valuable or important than others.

✓ or *	"As a result of the conflict, I felt . . ."	What That Feeling Sounds Like
	Invalidated	Who I am, what I think, what I do, or how I feel is not valued by my spouse.
	Unloved	My spouse doesn't love me anymore; my spouse has no affection or desire for me; my relationship lacks warm attachment, admiration, enthusiasm, or devotion.
	Dissatisfied	I will not experience satisfaction within the relationship; I will exist in misery for the rest of my life; I will not be pleased within my marriage; I feel no joy in my relationship.
	Taken advantage of	I will be cheated by my spouse; my partner will take advantage of me; my spouse will withhold something I need; I will feel like a doormat; I won't get what I want.
	Worthless or devalued	I am useless; my spouse fails to recognize my value and worth; I feel cheapened or undervalued in the relationship; I have little or no value to my spouse; my mate does not see me as priceless.
	Cheated	My spouse will take advantage of me; my spouse will withhold something I need; I won't get what I want.
	Not good enough	Nothing I do is ever acceptable, satisfactory, or sufficient for my spouse; I always have more "hoops" to jump through; I will never be able to meet my spouse's expectations of me; my efforts will never be enough.
	Unaccepted	My spouse does not accept me; my partner is not pleased with me; my spouse does not approve of me.

✓ or *	"As a result of the conflict, I felt . . ."	What That Feeling Sounds Like
	Judged	I am always being unfairly judged or misjudged; my spouse forms faulty or negative opinions about me; I am always being evaluated; my spouse does not approve of me.
	Humiliated	This marriage is extremely destructive to my self-respect or dignity.
	Ignored	My spouse will not pay attention to me; I feel neglected.
	Unimportant	I am not important to my spouse; I am irrelevant, insignificant, or of little priority to my spouse.
	Useless	I am of no use in my marriage; I am ineffective; I am not needed.
	Afraid of intimacy	I am afraid of opening up emotionally to my spouse; I will be hurt emotionally if I allow my spouse past my walls.
	Misunderstood	My spouse will fail to understand me correctly; my spouse will get the wrong idea or impression about me; I will be misinterpreted or misread.
	Misportrayed	My spouse has an inaccurate protrayal of me; I am misrepresented or represented in a false way; I am described in a negative or untrue manner; my spouse paints a wrong picture of me; my spouse has negative beliefs about me.
	Disrespected	I will be insulted; my spouse does not admire me; my spouse will have a low opinion of me; I will be disregarded; my spouse does not respect me; my spouse does not look up to me.

✓ or *	"As a result of the conflict, I felt . . ."	What That Feeling Sounds Like
	Out of control	My marriage will be wild, unruly, or hectic; my spouse will be unmanageable or uncontrollable; things will feel disorganized or in disorder.
	Alone	I will be by myself or on my own; I will be without help or assistance; I will be lonely; I will be isolated.
	Insignificant	I am irrelevant in the relationship; I am not necessary in my marriage; my spouse does not see me as an important part of our relationship.
	Unknown	My spouse will not know me; I will feel like a stranger to my spouse; I will be nameless or anonymous to my partner; I will be unfamilar to my spouse.
	As if I'm boring	There will be no passion in our marriage; my spouse perceives me as dull and dreary; our marriage is uninteresting; my spouse will believe that he or she knows everything there is to know about me; I feel as if we are just roommates; there will be no romantic feelings between us.
	Like a disappointment	I will be a letdown in the marriage; my spouse will be disppointed in me; my spouse will be disillusioned by me.
	Phony	My spouse will see me as fake or not genuine; my mate will believe that I'm a fraud, pretender, or an imposter; my spouse will perceive that I'm not who I say I am.
	Other:	

3. What do you *do* when you feel_____
[insert the most important feeling from question #2]? How do
you *react* when you feel that way? Identify your common *coping
strategies* to deal with that feeling. Check all that apply—but
"star" the most important coping behaviors:

✓ or *	"When I am in Conflict I . . ."	Explanation
	Withdraw	You avoid others or alienate yourself without resolution; you are distant; you sulk or use the silent treatment.
	Stonewall	You turn into a stone wall by not responding to your spouse.
	Escalate	Your emotions spiral out of control; you argue, raise your voice, fly into a rage.
	Emotionally shut down	You detach emotionally and close your heart towards your spouse; you "numb out"; you become devoid of emotion; you have no regard for others' needs or troubles.
	Pacify	You try to soothe, calm down, or placate your spouse; you try to get your spouse to not feel negative emotions.
	Try to earn love	You try to do more to earn others' love and care.
	Belittle	You devalue or dishonor someone with words or actions; you call your spouse names, use insults, ridicule, take potshots at, or mock him or her.
	Indulge in negative beliefs	You believe your spouse is far worse than is really the case; you see your spouse in a negative light or attribute negative motives to him or her; you see your spouse through a negative lens.
	Become arrogant	You posture yourself as superior, better than, or wiser than your spouse.

✓ or *	"When I am in Conflict I . . ."	Explanation
	Blame	You place responsibility on others, not accepting fault; you're convinced the problem is your spouse's fault.
	Become the innocent victim	You see your spouse as an attacking monster and yourself as put upon, unfairly accused, mistreated, or unappreciated.
	Control	You hold back, restrain, oppress, or dominate your spouse; you "rule over" your spouse; you talk over or prevent your spouse from having a chance to explain his or her position, opinions, or feelings.
	Use dishonesty	You lie, withhold information, or give out false impressions; you falsify your thoughts, feelings, habits, likes, dislikes, personal history, daily activities, or plans for the future.
	Withhold	You withhold your affections, feelings, sexual intimacy, or love from your spouse.
	Demand	You try to force your mate to do something, usually with implied threat of punishment if they refuse.
	Become annoying	You use irritating habits or activities to infuriate, annoy, upset, or to get on your spouse's nerves.
	Provoke	You intentionally aggravate, hassle, goad, or irritate your spouse.
	Isolate	You shut down and go into seclusion or into your "cave."
	Exaggerate	You make overstatements or enlarge your words beyond bounds or the truth; you make statements like "You always . . ." or "You never . . ."
	Throw tantrums	You have a fit of bad temper; you become irritable, crabby, or grumpy.

✓ or *	"When I am in Conflict I . . ."	Explanation
	Deny	You refuse to admit the truth or reality.
	Invalidate	You devalue your spouse; you do not appreciate who your partner is, what he or she feels or thinks or does.
	Maintain distressing thoughts	You replay the argument over and over; you don't stop thinking about the conflict or your spouse's frustrating or hurtful behavior.
	Independent	You become separate from your spouse in your attitude, behavior, and decision making.
	Rewrite history	You recast your earlier times together in a negative light; your recall of previous disappointments and slights becomes dramatically enhanced.
	Become defensive	Instead of listening, you defend yourself by providing an explanation; you make excuses for your actions.
	Become clingy	You develop a strong emotional attachment or dependence on your spouse; you hold tight to your spouse.
	Become passive-aggressive	You display negative emotions, resentment, and aggression in passive ways, such as procrastination, forgetfulness, and stubbornness.
	Avoid	You get involved in activities to avoid your spouse.
	Take care of others	You become responsible for others by giving physical or emotional care and support to the point you are doing everything for your spouse, and your partner does nothing to care for himself or herself.
	Become pessimistic	You become negative, distrustful, cynical, and skeptical in your view of your spouse and marriage.

✓ or *	"When I am in Conflict I . . ."	Explanation
	Act out	You engage in negative behaviors like drug or alcohol abuse, extramarital affairs, excessive shopping, or overeating.
	Go into fix-it mode	You focus almost exclusively on what is needed to solve the problem.
	Complain	You express unhappiness or make accusations.
	Criticize	You pass judgment, condemn, or point out your spouse's faults; you attack his or her personality or character.
	Strike out	You lash out in anger, become verbally or physically aggressive, possibly abusive.
	Manipulate	You control, influence, or maneuver your spouse for your own advantage.
	Get angry and enraged	You display strong feelings of displeasure or violent and uncontrolled emotions.
	Catastrophize	You use dramatic, exaggerated expressions to depict that the relationship is in danger or that it has failed.
	Pursue the truth	You try to determine what really happened or who is telling the truth.
	Judge	You negatively critique, evaluate, form an opinion, or conclude something about your spouse.
	Become selfish	You become more concerned with you and your interests, feelings, wants, or desires.
	Lecture	You sermonize, talk down to, scold, or reprimand your spouse.
	Cross-complain	You meet your spouse's complaint (or criticism) with an immediate complaint of your own, totally ignoring what your spouse has said.

✓ or *	"When I am in Conflict I . . ."	Explanation
	Whine	You express yourself by using a childish, high-pitched nasal tone and stress one syllable toward the end of the sentence.
	Use negative body language	You give a false smile, shift from side to side, or fold your arms across your chest.
	Use humor	You use humor as a way of not dealing with the issue at hand.
	Become sarcastic	You use negative or hostile humor, hurtful words, belittling comments, cutting remarks, or demeaning statements.
	Minimize	You assert that your spouse is overreacting to an issue; you intentionally underestimate, downplay, or soft-pedal the issue or how your spouse feels.
	Rationalize	You attempt to make your actions seem reasonable; you try to attribute your behavior to credible motives; you try to provide believable but untrue reasons for your conduct.
	Become indifferent	You are cold and show no concern.
	Abdicate	You give away responsibilities.
	Self-depreciate	You run yourself down.
	Agree, then disagree	You start out agreeing but end up disagreeing.
	Dump	You emotionally "vomit," unload, or dump on your spouse.
	Become a mind reader	You make assumptions about your spouse's private feelings, behaviors, or motives.
	Repeat	You become a broken record, repeating your own position incessantly instead of understanding your spouse's position.

✓ or *	"When I am in Conflict I . . ."	Explanation
	Argue	You argue about who is right and who is wrong; you debate whose position is the correct or right one.
	Abandon myself	You desert or neglect yourself; you take care of everyone except yourself.
	Become indignant	You believe that you deserve to be angry, resentful, or annoyed with your spouse because of what he or she did.
	Become stubborn	You will not budge from your position; you become inflexible or persistent.
	Act righteous	You make it a moral issue or argue about issues of morality or righteousness.
	Play dumb	You pretend not to understand or know what your spouse is talking about.
	Nag	You badger, pester, or harass your spouse to do something you want.
	Other:	

Notes

INTRODUCTION: MEET THE DOC
1. For those of you who don't know my dad, he has been speaking and writing about marriage for the past three decades.

CHAPTER 1—MARRIAGE 911
1. Josh McDowell and Bob Hostetler, *Josh McDowell's Handbook on Counseling Youth* (Dallas: Word, 1996).
2. U.S. Bureau of the Census, "Marriage, Divorce, and Remarriage in the 1990s," *Current Population Reports* (Washington, D.C.: U.S. Government Printing Office, 1992), 5.
3. John M. Gottman, "What Predicts Divorce?" Paper presented at the Erickson Foundation Conference, Dallas, Texas (March 1996).
4. U.S. Bureau of the Census, "Marriage, Divorce, and Remarriage in the 1990s," 4.
5. D. Mace and R. Mace, "Enriching Marriages: The Foundation Stone of Family Strength," in *Family Strengths: Positive Models for Family Life*, ed. Nick Stinnett et al. (Lincoln, Nebr.: University of Nebraska Press, 1980), 197–215.
6. Gottman, "What Predicts Divorce?"
7. See www.smalleymarriage.com.

CHAPTER 2—WHEN THE GOOD TIMES ROLL
1. Lee Robins and Darrel Regier, *Psychiatric Disorders in America: The Epidemiologic Catchment Area Study* (New York: Free Press, 1991), 334.
2. Steven Nock, *Marriage in Men's Lives* (New York: Oxford University Press, 1998).
3. Steven Sack and J. Ross Eshleman, "Marital Status and Happiness: A 17-Nation Study," *Journal of Marriage and the Family* 60 (1998): 527–536.
4. National Center for Health Statistics. *Health and Selected Socioeconomic Characteristics of the Family: United States, 1988–90* (PHS) (Washington D.C.: General Printing Office, 1997), 97–152.
5. Maggie Gallagher, "Marriage and Public Health," *Institute for American Values* (March 2001): 1.
6. Randy M. Page and Galen E. Cole, "Demographic Predictors of Self-Reported Loneliness in Adults," *Psychological Reports* 68 (1991): 939–945.
7. Linda J. Waite and Maggie Gallagher, *The Case for Marriage* (New York: Doubleday, 2000), 3.
8. Jane Mauldon, "The Effects of Marital Disruption on Children's Health," *Demography* 27 (1990): 431–446.

9. Deborah A. Dawson, "Family Structure and Children's Health and Well-being: Data from the 1988 National Health Interview Survey on Children's Health," *Journal of Marriage and the Family* 53 (1991): 573–584.

10. Ibid.

11. Ibid.

12. Ibid.

13. Waite and Gallagher, 3.

14. John Gottman, *Why Marriages Succeed or Fail* (New York: Simon & Schuster, 1994), 57.

15. Ibid.

16. Ibid.

17. David H. Olson and Amy Sigg, *Empowering Couples: Building on Your Strengths* (Minneapolis: Life Innovations, 2000); see also "National Survey of Marital Strengths," http://www.lifeinnovations.com/pdf/national_survey.pdf.

18. Nick Stinnett et al., *Fantastic Families* (West Monroe, La.: Howard Publishing, 1999), 10.

19. John M. Gottman and Nan Silver, *The Seven Principles for Making Marriage Work* (New York: Crown Publishers, 1999), 49.

20. For more information about the Covenant Marriage Movement, see the Web site at http://www.covenantmarriage.com.

21. Adapted from Dennis Shafer, busyhandsministries@lovejesus.net, an e-mail sent February 4, 2001.

CHAPTER 3—DESCENDING INTO MISERY

1. See Howard J. Markman, Scott M. Stanley, and Susan L. Blumberg, *Fighting for Your Marriage: Positive Steps for Preventing Divorce and Preserving a Lasting Love* (San Francisco: Jossey-Bass, 1994) and John Gottman, *Why Marriages Succeed or Fail* (New York: Simon & Schuster, 1994).

2. This self-test and scale were created for us by Scott Stanley and Howard Markman. Used by permission.

3. David H. Olson and Amy Sigg, *Empowering Couples: Building on Your Strengths* (Minneapolis: Life Innovations, 2000); see also "National Survey of Marital Strengths," http://www.lifeinnovations.com/pdf/national_survey.pdf.

CHAPTER 4—DOING A DESTRUCTIVE DANCE

1. D. Mace and R. Mace, "Enriching Marriages: The Foundation Stone of Family Strength," in *Family Strengths: Positive Models for Family Life,* ed. Nick Stinnett et al. (Lincoln, Nebr.: University of Nebraska Press, 1980), 197–215.

2. In high school, for example, my guidance counselor told me that I probably shouldn't go to college; he suggested that I pursue a trade instead. His words made me feel like a huge failure. My fear of failure is the core fear that plays the music to my Fear Dance.

CHAPTER 5—TAKING PERSONAL RESPONSIBILITY

1. Bill O'Hanlon, *Do One Thing Different* (New York: William Morrow and Company, 1999), 7.
2. Although God didn't evacuate his people in this way, he certainly could have. The story of Philip the evangelist describes an incident that looks very *Star Trek*ish indeed (see Acts 8:26-40).
3. *Merriam-Webster's Collegiate Dictionary*, 10th ed., s.v. "homeostasis."
4. Karen S. Peterson, "Unhappily Wed? Put Off Getting That Divorce," *USA Today*, 11 July 2002.
3. Ibid.

CHAPTER 6—LEARNING TO FORGIVE

1. William A. Meninger, *The Process of Forgiveness* (New York: Continuum, 1996), 33.

CHAPTER 7—HONORING EACH OTHER

1. Adapted from Father's Love Letter, http://www.FathersLoveLetter.com. Used by permission. Father Heart Communications, copyright © 1999.
2. The story is retold in Patricia McGerr, "Johnny Lingo's Eight-Cow Wife," *Readers' Digest* (February 1988): 138-141. The article originally appeared in the November 1965 edition of *Woman's Day*.
3. Adapted from Gary Smalley and Greg Smalley, *Winning Back Your Husband* (Nashville: Nelson, 1999), 1-2.
4. Stephen R. Covey, Roger Merrill, and Rebecca Merrill, *First Things First* (New York: Simon & Schuster, 1994), 265.

CHAPTER 8—TAKING CARE OF YOURSELF

1. S. I. McMillen, *None of These Diseases* (Westwood, N.J.: Revell, 1963).
2. Lawrence C. Katz and Manning Rubin, *Keep Your Brain Alive* (New York: Workman, 1999); Thedore I. Lidsky and Jay S. Schneider, *Brain Candy* (New York: Simon & Schuster, 2001).

CHAPTER 9—FINDING TREASURES IN TRIALS

1. Norman Vincent Peale, "Worth Fighting For," *Guideposts* (February 1977): 14.
2. These themes about negative thinking are adapted from Scott M. Stanley, et al., *A Lasting Promise: A Christian Guide to Fighting for Your Marriage* (San Francisco: Jossey-Bass, 1998).
3. For more information about Elliott's experiment, see http://www.horizonmag.com/4/jane-elliott.asp.
4. A woman handed me this quotation at a seminar. Although I have seen the quotation on Web sites, I do not know the print source of these words attributed to Charles Swindoll.
5. Mark Kane Goldstein, "Research Report: Annual Meeting of the Association for the Advancement of Behavior Therapy" (New York, October 1972), as quoted in Aaron T. Beck, *Love Is Never Enough: How*

Couples Can Overcome Misunderstandings, Resolve Conflicts, and Solve Relationship Problems Through Cognitive Therapy (New York: Harper & Row, 1988), 248.

CHAPTER 10—RESOLVING CONFLICT THROUGH COMMUNICATION

1. For more information about PREP, read Dr. Scott Stanley's book *A Lasting Promise: A Christian Guide to Fighting for Your Marriage* (San Francisco: Jossey-Bass, 1998), or visit his Web site at http://www.prepinc.com.

2. See Genesis 2:24; Matthew 19:5; 1 Corinthians 6:16; Ephesians 5:31.

3. Gary Smalley, *Secrets to Lasting Love: Uncovering the Keys to Life-Long Intimacy* (New York: Simon & Schuster, 2000).

4. John Gottman, *Why Marriages Succeed or Fail* (New York: Simon & Schuster, 1994).

5. The following studies found that communication methods such as LUV Talk produced very positive results in conflicts between parents and adolescents: S. L. Foster, R. J. Prinz, and K. D. O'Leary, "Impact of Problem-Solving Communication Training and Generalization Procedures on Family Conflict," *Child and Family Behavior Therapy* 5 (1983): 1–23; A. L. Robin, et al., "An Approach to Teaching Parents and Adolescents Problem-Solving Communication Skills: A Preliminary Report," *Behavior Therapy* 8 (1977): 639–643; A. L. Robin, "A Controlled Evaluation of Problem-Solving Communication Training with Parent-Adolescent Conflict," *Behavior Therapy* 12 (1981): 593–609; S. Stern, "A Group Cognitive-Behavioral Approach to the Management and Resolution of Parent-Adolescent Conflict" (Unpublished doctoral dissertation, University of Chicago, 1984).

CHAPTER 11—DEPENDING ON GOD'S POWER

1. Story taken from Steve Halliday, *Faith Is Stranger Than Fiction* (Green Forest, Ariz.: New Leaf Press, 2000), 48–49.

2. 1997 Gallup Poll commissioned by the National Association of Marriage Enhancement in Phoenix, Arizona.

3. HELLP is an acronym for hemolysis, elevated liver enzymes, and low platelet count.

CHAPTER 12—WHAT IS YOUR DREAM?

1. Remember the battle of Ai described in Joshua 7?

Relationships are in crisis.

Daily newspaper headlines give snapshots of people in deep relational crises:

- A mother abandons her family and children.
- A teenager starts a shooting spree over a deeply held grudge.
- Random terrorist attacks reveal ethnic and religious hatred.
- Divorce rates continue to skyrocket.

This is the tip of the iceberg.
Millions upon millions of men and women struggle with relationships with family, friends, coworkers, and neighbors.

→ YOU CAN MAKE A DIFFERENCE!
Join **The DNA of Relationships campaign,** and start to strengthen your own relationships—as well as relationships around you.

Log on to *dnaofrelationships.com* and receive

- Relationship resources that help you with difficult relationships
- Self-tests that help you discover the source of relationship conflict
- Study guides for small groups that want to have an impact on relationships
- Sermon ideas to highlight the importance of relationships to God
- *More information about upcoming DNA of Relationships books, videos, and seminars*

Go to the Web site, become a member, and start making a difference—today.

BOOKS IN
THE DNA OF RELATIONSHIPS
CAMPAIGN

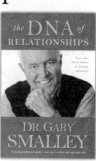

→ THE DNA OF RELATIONSHIPS FOR **MARRIAGE**

Have you ever wondered if your marriage could be better?

Dr. Greg Smalley can tell you how to
- discover your unique relationship dance
- break destructive relationship habits
- take personal responsibility
- forgive each other
- practice emotional communication

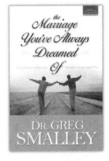

Dr. Greg Smalley directs the Smalley Marriage Institute, which offers marriage intensives for distressed couples. Couples come to the marriage intensives with broken and failed marriages, often ready to divorce the next week. Greg and his colleagues help couples understand the destructive relationship cycle that threatens their marriages—and how to heal the damage. Dr. Smalley bases his insights on five years of research conducted in his marriage intensives.

Look for the upcoming book *The DNA of Relationships for Couples* by Dr. Greg Smalley and Robert S. Paul.

→ THE DNA OF RELATIONSHIPS FOR **SINGLES**

What about dating relationships?

Check out Michael and Amy Smalley's *Don't Date Naked* book for straight talk about relationships for singles who are dating.

Michael and Amy Smalley regularly counsel singles and speak across the country about singles and dating. In this book, you'll find advice for both guys and girls, from Michael and Amy's differing perspectives.

We don't have to let MTV or FOX television shape our views of sex, dating, and relationships anymore. Read Michael and Amy's book to get a fresh perspective on what healthy dating is.

SMALLEY MARRIAGE INSTITUTE

THE SMALLEY MARRIAGE INSTITUTE (SMI) is a nonprofit ministry led by its founder and president, Dr. Greg Smalley. SMI has a team of highly trained marriage specialists who have one single mission: *to build, restore, and renew the promise of a great marriage.* Under the leadership of Robert S. Paul, the nationally recognized intensive programs have become a marriage "intensive care unit" or "ER" for couples who find themselves struggling in their marriage.

The SMI team's primary focus is to provide couples with insight and skills that can set them free from the barriers that keep them from having a great marriage. SMI is committed to helping couples create marriages that satisfy both spouses. These life-changing skills have dramatically changed the marriages of literally thousands of couples through our intensive programs, conferences, training workshops, and special events. These insights have been refined and translated by our professional team over the past several years and are made available to others in the following formats:

Intensives—Each week we see couples' relationships restored through our Marriage Intensive^{sm} program and Couples Intensive^{sm} program. Couples from all over the country come to our two-day and four-day intensives to work with two SMI marriage experts at either our Branson, Missouri, or Rome, Georgia, locations. Many of these couples are in crisis and very near divorce. Our research is suggesting that four months after attending one of our programs, over 93 percent of these couples are still together and reporting significant improvement in their marital satisfaction. SMI has established scholarship funds using gifts from donors and partners. These scholarship funds remove financial barriers, allowing more couples to attend and get the help they so desperately need.

Books, small-group curricula, and study guides—New, up-to-date resources are being contiually developed.

Professional training seminars—SMI offers training for therapists, counselors, clergy, and marriage mentors in order to give an overview of how to use and apply our model and intervention strategies.

Conferences—The Marriage Dance conference is designed to teach these principles to thousands of couples in an exciting enrichment format. It's our hope that every church, every small group, and every couple be equipped with these life-changing insights.

Special speaking—Our professional team is available to speak at special conferences and events. If you are interested in having one of our speakers speak at an event for your organization, please contact SMI for details.

To contact the Smalley Marriage Institute,
call toll-free at **866-875-2915** or
visit our Web site at **www.smalleymarriage.com.**

"Building, Restoring, and Renewing the Promise of a Great Marriage"

DR. GREG SMALLEY earned his doctorate in clinical psychology from Rosemead School of Psychology at Biola University in southern California. He also holds two master's degrees: one in counseling psychology from Denver Seminary and the other in clinical psychology from Rosemead School of Psychology.

Dr. Smalley is president of the Smalley Marriage Institute, a marriage and family ministry located in Branson, Missouri. He has taught relationship principles to thousands of couples and individuals throughout the world. He also has appeared on both television and radio programs, including *Focus on the Family* and *Hour of Power*. His publications include hundreds of articles on relationship and parenting issues for *Marriage Partnerships, Christian Parenting Today, ParentLife, Living with Teenagers, Shine, Homes of Honor,* and *HonorBound*. He has coauthored several books, including *The DNA of Relationships, Men's Relational Toolbox, Bound by Honor, Winning Your Wife Back, Winning Your Husband Back,* and *Life Lines: Communicating with Your Teen*.

Dr. Smalley maintains a counseling practice that specializes in marriage intensives, a resource to couples in crisis.

Greg and his wife, Erin, have three children: two daughters, Taylor and Maddy, and a son, Garrison. The Smalleys live in Branson, Missouri.

Notes

Notes

Notes

Notes

Notes

Notes

Notes

Notes

Notes